The English Legal System

Course Companion

&

Revision Guide

AS level Law

By
Jo Smillie, LLB(Hons)

The author would like to thank:
➢ OCR for the permission to use OCR specimen materials and examination questions
➢ Walter Dodds BA (Hons), Solicitor, for suggestions and proofreading

The law is stated as I believe it to be on 1st July 2007

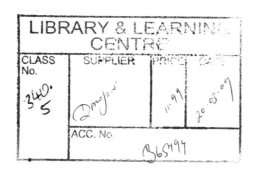
Order this book online at www.trafford.com/06-2525
or email orders@trafford.com

Most Trafford titles are also available at major online book retailers.

Note for Librarians: A cataloguing record for this book is available from Library and Archives Canada at www.collectionscanada.ca/amicus/index-e.html

ISBN: 978-1-4251-0767-3

We at Trafford believe that it is the responsibility of us all, as both individuals and corporations, to make choices that are environmentally and socially sound. You, in turn, are supporting this responsible conduct each time you purchase a Trafford book, or make use of our publishing services. To find out how you are helping, please visit www.trafford.com/responsiblepublishing.html

Our mission is to efficiently provide the world's finest, most comprehensive book publishing service, enabling every author to experience success. To find out how to publish your book, your way, and have it available worldwide, visit us online at www.trafford.com/10510

 **Trafford** PUBLISHING™ www.trafford.com

North America & international
toll-free: 1 888 232 4444 (USA & Canada)
phone: 250 383 6864 ♦ fax: 250 383 6804 ♦ email: info@trafford.com

The United Kingdom & Europe
phone: +44 (0)1865 722 113 ♦ local rate: 0845 230 9601
facsimile: +44 (0)1865 722 868 ♦ email: info.uk@trafford.com

10 9 8 7 6 5 4

CONTENTS

Outline of new AS __Unit 2__ examination paper:
Sources of Law   [G142]
For OCR exam board

The exam paper will include 2 data questions:
Each containing 3 parts:

- a) explain …   for 12 marks   [**AO1** knowledge]
- b) apply law to 3 scenarios …   for 15 marks (3x5)   [**AO2** application]
- c) i explain, describe ….   for 15 marks [**AO1** knowledge]
       c) ii discuss …   for 12 marks [**AO2** evaluation]

- 6 marks across the question for AO3 (grammar, logical sequence, structure of answers)

Students must answer 1 question
Answering all parts of that question
 ➤ structure answers to include references to the source materials provided
 ➤ [this is a skills-based paper, hence the importance of referring to the source material provided]

The exam is for one hour
A total of 60 raw marks for this paper
Forming 40% of the AS law examination

The questions are based upon the following topics:

- **Legislation**
- **Delegated legislation**
- **Law Reform**
- **Statutory Interpretation**
- **Judicial Precedent**
- **European Law**

The questions may not be based solely upon one of the above topics – but could include two topics:

e.g.   a)   explain an aspect of European Law
       b)   Apply delegated legislation to 3 scenarios
       c) i   Describe one type of delegated legislation
       c) ii   Evaluate delegated legislation

 ➤ [see page 11 for a specimen example of the new specification question for this paper.]

 ➤ [See page 42 for outline of the OCR AS unit 1 paper: English Legal System]

○ *You need to know:*

- ○ Doctrine of Separation of Powers, & Supremacy of Parliament
- ○ Process of making an Act of Parliament (Legislation; law)
- ○ Different types of Bill (proposals for Acts)

○ *Need to be able to comment upon:*

- ○ Process of Bill becoming an Act
- ○ Different types of Bills
- ○ Advantages and disadvantages of Parliament making law
- ○ Reform to House of Lords
- ○ **Link with topic of delegated legislation; law reform; EC law.**

* *

PARLIAMENT:

- **House of Lords**
  - ○ Hereditary and life **Peers**
  - ○ Judges (Law Lords)
  - ○ Senior bishops in Church of England
    [note current proposal for reform, below]
- **House of Commons**
  - ○ **elected** by the public
  - ○ Cabinet = Gov. of the day – democratic law making
  - ○ Mainstay for making law
- **Monarch[Queen]**

Today, legislative process is dominated by the Government

- Hence the **major function of Parliament is the scrutiny of the Government.**
  - Gladstone: Parliament is " a constant critic of the government"
  - **Government are elected:** idea of democratic law making.
  - Law and politics entwined!

SUPREMACY of Parliament:

- *EC law aside*: Parliament are the supreme law makers in our English legal system:
- **Parliament can make or break any law it likes**
  - ○ *(external and political pressures place restraints on the kind of legislation Parliament actually passes – "a political football")*
- **Their law (Act / Statute) is supreme**
  - ○ judges must apply legislation   [legislation takes precedence over case law]

Proposed REFORM of House of Lords:

To the LEGISLATIVE CHAMBER of the House of Lords:
An Issue of ability/suitability of vast number of peers who inherit title; [unlike life peers who "earn" title] yet are able to sit in House of Lords and propose / debate legislation. In **1999** there were 1,110 members in House of Lords. By passing the **House of Lords Act 1999**, the Labour Government reduced the number of hereditary peers from 750 to 92 – **beginning of reform of the House. Wakeham Commission** – reported in 2000 and **recommended** reforming the House: 20%be elected / 20% be selected by an appointments commission /
remainder to be nominated by political parties; in proportion to their share of the vote in the previous election.   **This set out in Lords Reform White Paper – Dec 2001** however is still the subject of controversial debate and hence **this reform has not been implemented.** *Arguably resulting in a more party political House of Lords – Raising question of whether such a political House could carry out its main purpose of checking and balancing the politically elected first chamber of Parliament – namely the House of Commons.*

Process of making an Act of Parliament: *legislation*

Pre-legislative procedure:
Consultation <u>On major matters</u>, government will issue:

GREEN PAPER
Consultation document on possible new law
Usually issued by Minister with responsibility for that matter.
Use of Green Papers introduced 1967 (Labour Gov.)
Interested parties are then invited to send comments to the
relevant Gov. dept. who consider the comments; which may
lead to changes in the proposal.   <u>Then issue:</u>
WHITE PAPER   Government's firm proposals for
new law.   **These proposals will be drafted into the Bill.**

Create a Bill:
A **Bill is the proposal for new legislation**, which if **it successfully completes all stages**, in **both Houses of Parliament**, and receives **Royal Assent, then it becomes an Act – primary legislation.**

There are 3 types of Bill
Differences denote who is proposing new law, and whom it will affect:

PUBLIC BILLS
- Proposed by the **cabinet - matters of public policy.**
- They propose to change the **general law of the whole country, or a large section of it.**
<u>Public Bills which have led to Acts of Parl.:</u>
PACE 1984
Access to Justice Act 1999
Powers of Criminal Courts (Sentencing) Act 2000
- The **bulk of primary legislation** is introduced by Public bills.
- **These Bills often come after a Green and White paper**

PRIVATE BILLS
- Proposed by **local authority** or **public corporation.**
- Propose to change law **to affect the group proposing new law.**
- *for example a local authority seeking the legal right to build a bridge or road.*
<u>Public Bills which have led to Acts of Parl.:</u>
University College London Act 1996 passed in order to combine 3 medical teaching institutions.

  .

PRIVATE MEMBERS' BILLS
- proposed by an **individual MP.**
- Propose to change law to **affect the whole country – or small number of people / particular body.**
- **BUT not all are debated:**
- *Every Parliamentary session MP's enter ballot, 20 names are drawn to present their Bill to Parliament. but, due to a limited time to debate these bills – usually Fridays – only a few (6 or 7) get debated.*
- *Note, back-bench MP's can try to introduce a private member's bill through the 10 minute rule – a 10 minute speech to try to gain support for introducing the Bill.*
Although few such Bills become Acts, some have produced important laws
– for example:
Abortion Act 1967 which legalised abortion.
Computers Misuse Act 1990.

The bulk of Bills are in the form of Public Bills,
Introduced by the government.

Bills are written by Parliamentary Counsel –
lawyers who are civil servants.

Process for Bill to become an Act: *legislation*

1. Possible Green & White paper
2. Bill drafted
3. **Bill introduced & debated in each House of Parliament**
4. Bill receives Royal Assent to become an Act of Parliament – [primary legislation]

- **All** types of Bill must pass through **each House** of Parliament (Commons / Lords)
- The **same procedure** is followed in each House, which **involves**:
    - **two main debates** on the **principles and a final vote.**
    - **one debate - on the words / detail - by a select committee.**
- The Bill **may start in either House first**
    - with exception of finance Bills which must start in the House of Commons first.

Procedure – through each House of Parliament: *5 stages*

First Reading   **Formal introduction of Bill** into the House
Title and main aims read out, but no debate

Second Reading   **Main debate** on Bill's **principles**
"catch Speaker's eye" to speak in the debate
[Speaker of House controls who speaks in the House]

VOTES
Bill must pass each stage:
Be voted "aye" to consider Bill further.
Members of the House call "aye" or "no" & votes counted
Or, votes counted as members walk through "aye" door or "no" door into the House.

Committee Stage   **Clause by clause consideration** of the Bill
by select committee of the House of Commons.
Consider wording: whether it achieves main principles / aims
[In House of Commons: Committee of MP's chosen for each Bill; Group of MP's with knowledge
of (interest in) the Bill. [Finance Bills require whole House sits as committee]
In House of Lords, this stage, if occurs, is usually by whole House sitting as committee.

Royal Assent -
Monarch's approval
mere formality as
the Monarch rarely
refuses. *Queen Anne was last monarch to refuse consent: in 1707, refusal to assent to the Scottish Militia Bill.* **Bill becomes Act [law] at midnight on day receives Royal Assent;** but **may not come into force until a later date** (if future implementation date; for all or part of Act – is stated in the Act.)

Report Stage   **Committee reports back to House:**
on any recommendations for amendments to the Bill
for the House to debate such amendments
(if Committee not suggest any amendments, Bill goes straight to Third Reading.)

Third Reading   **Final debate** on the Bill
Unlikely to fail at this stage, in fact is not always a debate.
final vote for the Bill through the House:
[final vote on whether to accept or reject the Bill]
There will be **vote at the end of each of the 5 stages**, as to whether the members wish
the Bill to be considered further, or not. The final vote for the Bill to be "passed by the House"
occurs in the Third Reading. **If final vote is "aye" [yes] then the Bill will be introduced to the other House of Parliament.**
When the Bill has been successfully passed through both Houses of Parliament it must receive
Royal Assent by the Monarch in order to become an Act of Parliament.

House of Lords   Bill goes through the 3 Readings (same as in House of Commons) – any amendments are then
considered by House of Commons. The House of Lords **only has the power to delay a Bill becoming an Act:** *Under
the Parliament Acts of 1911 & 1949 if the House of Lords reject the Bill (vote "no") then the Bill can still become law if
in the next Parliamentary session it successfully passes back through the House of Commons.* However, rarely needed to
invoke this power as non-elected **House of Lords usually adheres to its function of refining, adding to proposal for
law made by the democratically elected House of Commons.** Only been used 4 times e.g. Hunting Act 2004 where
House of Lords did oppose the House of Commons.

Pressures on Parliament to make new law: *legislation*

Most new law arises from government policy:
- Government's **election manifesto**
  - Promises of future reform, made by the party when on election campaign
- **Queen's Speech** – at the start of every Parliamentary session
  - Government announces reforms it intends to make

Or, **in order for Government to enact European Law**
- Create an Act in order to give effect to European Law (create the rights / obligations)

Or, **in response to suggestions of Law Reform agencies**
- [e.g. reform of rules concerning legal funding & advice]

Or, **in response to pressure from media / groups in society**
- [e.g. Disability Discrimination Act 1995 (rights for the disabled)

Or, **in response to a tragic event**
- [e.g. following "9/11": Twin Towers terrorist attack in New York, Parliament created Anti-Terrorism, Crime and Security Act 2001.]

> See pages 28, 30 – Law Reform, for more details on the influences upon Parliament to make law.

Evaluation of Legislation:

Disadvantages:
- **Time taken to make law:**
  - It takes several months to go through the 5 stages in both Houses of Parliament
  - A slow method of creating law
- **Lack of accessibility:**
  - Difficulty in finding out which Acts / sections are in force
  - Difficulty in finding out all Acts on a given topic (original Act and later amendments)
- **Lack of clarity:**
  - Obscure and complex language used
    – which results in many cases of statutory interpretation:
    To find the meaning of words in Act in order to apply the law to the facts of the case.
  - Over-elaborate detail is used – as draftsmen try to cover every possible future situation the Act could be applied to.

Advantages:
- **Democratic law making process**
  - Publicly elected government - "law for the people, by the people"
- **Law is debated**
  - scrutinised and amended;
  - publicised through debates.
- **Enables consultation with interested parties**
  - For major government policy through green & white papers.

Exam Questions on Legislation

Questions tend to focus upon the following:
1. Describing the process by which Bills become Acts of Parliament.
2. Describing and comparing the 3 types of Bill
3. Explaining the terms "Green Paper" and "White Paper"

This topic is usually questioned along with other topics of:
1. Law Reform (and legislation) – [see page 27]
2. Delegated Legislation (and legislation) – [see page 5]
3. and possibly: EC law (and legislation) – [see page 31]

New specification specimen question: [see page 11 for example of a question]
Question with 3 parts: a, b, c, which must be answered with reference to the source (printed material) provided - total of 60 marks.
- a)   12 marks … AO1 … "describe, explain …"
- b)   15 marks … AO2 … 3 problem scenarios to apply law to
- c)   27 marks ….in total, split as follows:
  - c(i) 15 marks – AO1 - "describe"; & c(ii) 12 marks – AO2- " discuss, comment upon"

[6 marks for AO3 which is global for the paper] – a total of 60 raw marks [40% of total AS Law]

- ○ **You need to know:**
    - ○ What delegated legislation is, and why we have it
    - ○ Different types of delegated legislation [statutory instrument / bylaw / Order in Council]
    - ○ Control of delegated legislation by:
        - ▪ by Parliament and by the courts (judicial review)

- ○ **Need to be able to comment upon:**
    - ○ Similarities and differences between the 3 types of delegated legislation
    - ○ Advantages and disadvantages of delegated legislation
    - ○ Effectiveness of control of delegated legislation, by Parliament & by the courts.
    - ○ **Link with topic of legislation, and with topic of law reform, and with topic of EC law.**

* *

Delegated legislation is:

- a **series of laws** [secondary legislation]
- Made by **a person / body <u>other than Parliament</u>**
- But **under the <u>authority of Parliament</u>**

> Parliament enact the POLICY in an Act.
>
> Government departments and local authorities create the DETAIL necessary to bring the policy into force.

> If an Act contains a section delegating power to make law to others it is called:
> a <u>Parent Act</u>
> [or an Enabling Act]
> (e.g. AJA 1999 delegated power to Lord Chancellor to alter various aspects of legal funding)

Parliament delegates the power to make law due to its lack of:
- **time** to make all the law necessary
- **local knowledge** needed for laws affecting a locality
    e.g. bylaws
- **technical knowledge** needed for the detailed rules
    e.g. building regulations

There are 3 types of delegated Legislation
Differences denote who is making it, and whom it will affect:

Statutory Instruments:
- law countrywide
- made by ministers of government departments rules and regulations for areas under their responsibility.

- It is a **major method of law making** – some 3,000 are brought into force each year.
- The enabling Act will specify whether the statutory instrument must be laid before Parliament: either by affirmative resolution (involving some debate) or through negative resolution (no debate).
 e.g. *Health and Safety (Display Screen Equipment) Regulations 1992* .

Bylaws:
- law in local area
- made by local authorities to cover local matters and sometimes by public corporations and certain companies for matters within their jurisdiction <u>which involve the public.</u>
Involve matters of only local concern, *e.g.*
Parking restrictions or dogs fouling footpaths, or in the case of corporations, restrictions on the behaviour of people who use their services, eg. Smoking on the underground.

Orders in Council:
- law countrywide in times of emergency
- made by :
Usually drafted by a government department and **approved by the Queen and Privy Council** – by virtue of Emergency Powers Act 1920.
Used during time of war, OR
When Parliament is not sitting,
WHEN need to make law quickly
E.g. the fuel crisis of September 2000 saw Parliament put the Privy Council on alert had the need to pass emergency legislation arisen.

Control of Delegated Legislation   *- by Parliament*

Main method of control: **Wording of enabling Act**
The enabling Act itself lays down the nature and scope of the delegated powers – hence control through wording of Act: not giving too wide delegating power.

Second method: **Resolution Procedure**
Some delegated legislation may be required (by enabling Act) to be laid before Parliament before it becomes law – some S.I's – either by affirmative or by negative resolution. Explain these:
Affirmative : only becomes law if affirmed – motion approving it is passed within a specified period. Negative: becomes law automatically unless MP puts down a motion to annul the delegated legislation within 40 days – i.e. rejects the DL

Third method: **Scrutiny Committees**
1. **Delegated Powers Scrutiny Committee**,
   - established in 1993 in House of Lords – to look at Bills delegating legislative power (i.e. Bills which will become enabling Acts), to consider whether the legislative powers is being delegated inappropriately – open to possible abuse. Reports findings to Committee stage of process of Bill, but has no power to amend Bill.

2. The Scrutiny Committee [**Joint Select Committee on Statutory Instruments**]
   - formed 1973, to review all statutory instruments but on technical not policy basis. Refers back to Parliament usually if statutory instruments imposes tax or charge, appears to have retrospective effect, or goes beyond powers granted in enabling Act. Again, can only report findings, not amend.

Fourth method: **If Parliament requires consultation – (through enabling Act)**
Often an enabling Act will make consultation with certain parties obligatory. These parties consulted may include advisory bodies, experts or other interested parties e.g. in cases of road traffic regulations ministers are likely to seek the advice of police, motoring organisation, vehicle manufacturers and local authorities – consultation, helping to avoid abuse of power, helping with control of delegated legislation.

Summary:
All statutes
- limited control by Parliament through the wording of the Act (Statute), and through Delegated Powers Scrutiny Committee checking enabling Bills.

S.I's
- through Resolution Procedure, and
- Scrutiny Committee

S.I's & Bylaws
- If Consultation requirement

Conclusion:

Parliaments powers to control delegated legislation are fairly limited.

However to a certain extent, such powers to intervene should be limited otherwise the object of delegating legislative power is defeated (lack of parliamentary time – see above).

The criticism of lack of control is one which grows with the growing use of delegated legislation. Main criticism: stems from fact that delegated legislation is made by non-elected bodies – that it **takes Law making away from the democratically elected House of Commons**, *which is, to a certain extent, acceptable provided there is sufficient control. The Legislative and Regulatory Reform Bill 2006 proposes to increase the use of delegated legislation – see page 10.*

All delegated legislation must conform to the limits laid down expressly (or impliedly) by the enabling Act; if those limits are exceeded the validity of the piece of delegated legislation may be challenged in the courts.

Once made, delegated legislation can be **challenged in the courts** on the **grounds** that it **is <u>ultra vires</u>** – that it goes beyond the law

1.   **beyond the powers** granted by Parl. in the enabling Act - **substantial ultra vires;**   or
2.   **not followed procedure** laid down by Parl. in the enabling Act - **procedural ultra vires**

or   3.   that the piece of delegated legislation **is unreasonable.**

> *The court will presume (unless enabling Act expressly allows it) that NO power is delegated to levy taxes, or to allow sub-delegation.*

Substantive Ultra Vires
Subject matter lies beyond the power / scope laid down in the enabling Act

- As seen in:

Cure & Deeley Ltd case (1962),
Held: The Enabling Act did not give the commissioners the power to determine the amount of tax due where a tax return was submitted late. **The enabling Act merely empowered them to collect such tax and not to decide what amount they saw fit.** High court declared regulation void (not law).

- As seen in:

Welfare of Immigrants case (1996)
Social security benefits for asylum seekers was costing over £2 million a year so the Secretary for Social Security enacted delegated legislation (a regulation) stating benefits would no longer be available to those who sought asylum **after** they had entered the UK – must do so immediately upon entry. **Held: the regulation was void for substantive ultra vires as the enabling Act cannot have intended to enable the Minister to take away the right to benefits for asylum seekers, clearly granted under a different Act of Parliament.**

A controversial decision because the regulation (delegated legislation) itself had been approved by Parliament under the resolution system. Declaring the regulation void was seen as challenging Parliament.

Procedural Ultra Vires
Not followed a procedure laid down in the enabling Act

- As seen in:

Aylesbury Mushroom case (1972)
The enabling Act required minister of labour to "consult any organisation … appearing to him to be representative of substantial number of employees engaged in the activity concerned." **Minister,** in setting up a training board (by statutory instrument), **did not consult** the Mushroom Growers Association [which accounted for 85% of all mushroom growers]. **Held: The Statutory Instrument was void (not law) in regard to the Mushroom Growers Association, but was valid for all others, eg farmers, because the minister had consulted the Farmers Union**

This challenge is under a procedure known as: **Judicial Review** in QBD of the High Court. Challenge must be made **within 3 months** of the time when the grounds for application arose. ALSO **Leave must be granted** by single judge in High Court. The **person making the challenge must have** "sufficient interest in the matter to which the application relates." – *locus standi*

- The above are for **direct challenges**.
- The challenge **can also be made indirectly by raising ultra vires as a defence to proceedings.** *As seen in the Aylesbury Mushroom case – raised by Mushroom Growers Association as defence to being sued for contravening the statutory instrument.*

Unreasonableness

Delegated legislation will be declared void where it is :

So unreasonable that no reasonable public body could have reached the same decision.

- **This is known as the Wednesbury principle.**
(established in Associated Provincial Picture Houses Ltd v Wednesbury Corporation (1948)).

As described by Lord Diplock, in *Council of Civil Service Unions v Minister for the Civil Service (1984)*
"a decision which is so outrageous in its defiance of logic or accepted
moral standard that no sensible person … could have arrived at it."

- If declared unreasonable by the court, the decision will be held outside the public body's power: ultra vires for unreasonableness.

- As seen in: **_Strictland v Hayes Borough Council (1896)_**

A Bylaw prohibiting singing or reciting of any obscene song/ballad and use of obscene language generally, was **held ultra vires and void for unreasonableness** because it was too wide in that it covered acts done in private as well as in public. The behaviour of county council in exercising power was argued to be unreasonable.

- The **Principle of unreasonableness extended in:**
R v Derbyshire County Council, ex p Times Supplements (1990)
The Times challenged the DCC's decision to stop advertising its educational posts in the Times publications, after Sunday Times had published 2 articles accusing council of improper and legally dubious behaviour. **Held: council had been motivated by bad faith and vindictiveness and this was an abuse of power.**

In the procedure of Judicial Review, judges "review" decisions (or refusal to make decisions) of inferior courts and tribunals, public bodies and officials. Therefore, **judicial review allows the court to supervise the workings of a wide range of decision-making bodies – to some extent to control delegated legislation.**

> *Lord Woolf defined the role of judicial review as balancing the need of the rights of the individual to be treated fairly; with the rights of government at local and national level, to do what they have been elected to do.*

Court options:

If the court find that the piece of delegated legislation is ultra vires, **it can declare the delegation legislation to be VOID**   [not law].

Either   The **ENTIRE** piece of delegated legislation

Or   **PART** of it – i.e. "sever", leaving remainder as valid law.

Or   **void as to APPLICANT**, but valid for others –[as seen in Aylesbury Mushroom case above.]

Remedies: if the delegated legislation is found to be ultra vires:

High Court has **3 perogative orders** which **can** be used when application for judicial review is successful – all orders are discretionary – therefore even if public body behaved illegally, the court may still refuse a remedy. Certiorari / mandamus / prohibition: public law orders, [from the idea that the monarch controls officials].   **[Plus, can award private law remedies of damages, injunction, declaration]**

Certioriari _"we wish to be informed" This **order quashes (nullifies) an ultra vires decision** – for example, used to quash refusal of a mandatory student grant	Mandamus "**we command**" - note is often used with certioriari order. **This order to do something: orders that powers be used properly.** eg to hear an appeal that a tribunal has previously refused to hear, or to provide accounts
Prohibition **used to prevent public body from acting unlawfully in the future.**	

Criticism of Judicial Review:

1   **need leave to apply from courts and within 3 months!**
No other first instant court action requires such leave. This is said to discourage ordinary people who wish to pursue an action – further, they may be unaware of their rights within the 3 month time-limit.

2   **Wednesbury Rules** – no general unfairness ground. It is **difficult to prove** that a decision is "so unreasonable" that no public body could have come to it.

3   **Political role of judges** – many cases involve challenge to decisions made by government minister / local council – this requires judge to make political decisions – this goes **against separation of powers doctrine.** [see page 69]

4   **As method of control over delegated legislation judicial review is very limited**:
A case must come before the court. Further, it is difficult for the court to limit wide discretionary powers given by Parliament. E.g. the Secretary of State had power to "do all things as appear to him to be necessary or expedient" to enable council tenants to buy their council houses – under Housing Act 1980.

EVALUATION of   DELEGATED LEGISLATION:

Advantages - why we have delegated legislation

- **Speed** – quicker to enact than an Act of Parliament. (& Orders in Council enable quick response to an emergency)
- **Lack of Parliamentary time** to make all legislation necessary
- Legislation made by those with **specialist and/or local knowledge** (technical problems debated by experts)
- **Allows flexibility** – quick to enact and can be easily revoked.
- **Bylaws** enable laws for a locality to reflect local interests

Disadvantages

Main criticism of DL is that it takes law-making away from the democratically elected House of Commons; allowing non-elected people to make law. This is acceptable provided there is sufficient control –but, control by Parliament and by Courts is limited – However, to a certain extent such powers to intervene should be limited otherwise the object of delegating legislative power is defeated!
- **Lack of democratic involvement**
- **Overuse**
- **Sub-delegation**
- **Lack of control**
- **Lack of debate and publicity**
- (delegated legislation) **Can be as complex as legislation**; often requiring statutory interpretation

---

Comparison of legislative process of Act / Delegated legislation:

	Act	Delegated Legislation
Time to become law	longer	quicker
Debate	opportunity for	no opportunity for
Democratic process	yes	no (statutory instrument often by single minister)
Court ability to question	no	yes (challenge validity in Judicial Review)

Legislative and Regulatory Reform Bill 2006: [currently before the House of Lords] **gives government ministers greater powers to make law : to make, repeal or replace any legislation in any way that an Act of Parliament may do, and to amend or abolish any rule of common law, or codify common law rules if necessary to implement Law Commission recommendations. The limitations are: cannot increase taxation, nor create new offence with penalty greater than 2 years in prison.** Such delegated legislation only requires resolution procedure before Parliament (& possibly consultation) – along with explanation that "safeguard" conditions are met, which include clarifying that the new legislation does not remove any persons "legitimate expectation" of rights / freedoms. The controversy surrounding this Bill concerns the order making power of the Bill - a Bill some constitutional experts are already calling "the Abolition of Parliament Bill"

Exam Question on Delegated Legislation:

1 (a) Describe and explain the three types of delegation.

(b) (i) Explain for what reasons delegated legislation can be challenged in the courts;

(ii) Describe the orders that can be made if that challenge is successful.

(c) Discuss the main advantages and disadvantages of delegated legislation.

(d) Suggest whether the following might be subject to challenge in the courts:

(i) Using powers of discretion given under a statute for applications for asylum the Home Secretary introduced a statutory instrument preventing applications for asylum from any immigrant entering from Asian, African, or Latin American county.

(ii) An Act allows the Home Secretary to introduce statutory instruments to to provide emergency accommodation for asylum seekers after first consulting local authorities and holding meetings with local residents. The Home Secretary responding, to a sudden influx of asylum seekers, erects a camp near to a town without consulting the local council or holding a public meeting.

OCR AS Level Law, June 2001, Q1

Exam Question on Delegated Legislation and Legislation:

1 (a) Briefly describe the process by which Acts of Parliament are passed.

(b) Describe the controls exercised over delegated legislation by both Parliament and the courts.

(c) Discuss the statement that "Despite the controls over delegated legislation, the reality is that effective supervision is difficult".

(d) Identify and explain which *type* of delegated legislation would be most appropriate to introduce law relating to:

(i) The use of mobile phones on trains;
(ii) The implementation of regulations outlined in an enabling act;
(iii) Emergency measures to be taken in times of war.

OCR AS Level Law, January 2003, Q1

[example of new specification question is on next page – 11]

New specification specimen question:
On delegated legislation and European law:

Question with 3 parts: a, b, c, which must be answered <u>with reference</u> to the
<u>source</u> *(printed material) provided - total of 60 marks.*

<u>SOURCE B</u>:
The Health and Safety (Display Screen Equipment) Regulations 1992:
Some important definitions:

▪ **Display Screen Equipment used at workstations** *includes* computer monitors. Screens
  showing mainly TV or film picture are *not* covered.
▪ **Users**: Uses the display screen equipment more or less daily and for continuous spells of
  an hour or more at a time.

The Regulations:
Regulation 1: requires every employer to perform a suitable and sufficient assessment of
workstations to assess any health and safety risks and to take action to reduce those risks to
the lowest extent possible.
Regulation 2: requires employers to plan the activities of those using workstations so that
Daily work is periodically interrupted by breaks or activity changes. These could be informal
Breaks away from the screen for a short period each hour.
Regulation 3: gives users the opportunity to have an appropriate eye and eyesight test as
Soon as practicable after requesting one and at regular intervals thereafter. The costs will be
met by the employer.

                                                    Adapted from the Regulations.

Question: answer all parts.

(a)   Briefly explain with examples, the terms 'vertical direct effect' **and**
        'horizontal direct effect'. [12]

(b)   Apply the content of The Health and Safety (Display Screen Equipment) Regulations
        1992, in **Source B**, to each of the situations described below:

        (i)   Mario is about to start a new job as librarian in a small school. The job will require
                 occasional use of a computer monitor. The Deputy Head is also the school Health
                 and Safety Officer and is anxious to comply with all relevant legislation.   [5]

        (ii)   Amir works as a telephone-sales representative. His regular daily work requires long
                 periods of sustained concentration as he transfers information from customers onto a
                 computer system. He is finding it increasingly difficult to sustain his concentration.
                 [5]

        (iii)   Julie works as a receptionist in a busy office. Her daily work involves monitoring a
                 TV screen (fed from security cameras) and constant use of a computer monitor to
                 perform a variety of functions. She has started to suffer with blurred vision. [5]

(ci)   Describe with examples the nature of statutory instruments and the process of bringing
        them into force. [15]

(cii)   Discuss the advantages and disadvantages of delegated legislation. [12]

        OCR AS Level Law, Q1 specimen paper G142QP
[6 marks for AO3 which is global for the paper] – a total of 60 raw marks **[40% of total AS Law marks]**

o *You need to know:*
  o What statutory interpretation is
  o Different approaches judges can take to statutory interpretation
  o Different aids the judges can use in relation to the different approaches
    ▪ In particular: Hansard and Rules of Language

o *Need to be able to comment upon:*
  o Similarities and differences between the different approaches
  o Advantages and disadvantages of statutory interpretation
    o Link with: separation of powers doctrine / do judges make law – should they?
  o Impact of joining European Union upon judges use of the approaches
  o **Link with topics of legislation, delegated legislation, law reform and EC law.**
  *

The role of judges is to apply the law to the facts of the case before them in order to resolve the dispute (civil or criminal). **Statutory interpretation is the approach that the judges have developed over time, to find the exact meaning of words or phrases in legislation** (including delegated legislation and EC law) – in order to fulfil their role.

Whether an individual can rely upon a right given in legislation, or is guilty of a crime (as stated in legislation) depends upon whether their action falls within the meaning of the words in the legislation. You will see that this can often depend upon how the judge interprets that legislation:

There are **4 approaches** that the judges can use to find the meaning of the words/phrases in legislation – it is their **discretion** which to use. **Different approaches can lead to different results – hence the outcome of the case can depend upon the choice of approach the judge takes in interpreting the legislation.** Whichever approach the judge uses, he can use internal and external **aids** to help him find either the **meaning of the word, or the intention of Parliament.**

Approaches
- 3 approaches (principles) developed by judges, and 1 approach inherited from EC law.
- In effect these are a set of 'rules' that judges follow in order to find the meaning of words/phrases in legislation.
- It is up to the judge which approach he uses – judge's discretion.
  - The **Literal** Rule
  - The **Golden** Rule
  - The **Mischief** Rule
  - The **Purposive** Approach

> **Legislation often needs interpreting:**
> **Broad terms are often used:**
> e.g. "vehicles" – does this include skateboards, motorised scooters?
> **Words are left out in the belief they would be implied:**
> e.g. "men with beards or moustaches are prohibited from parks" – does this mean a ban for men with both? – (and/or).
> **Errors occur in drafting and printing of legislation**
> **Legislation cannot foresee all future events / technology.**
> **Ambiguity is included due to politically contentious nature of the legislation.**

Aids
These are classified as either:
Internal   - within the Act
External   - outside the Act
"Aids" are where the judge can go to gain help in finding the meaning of words or the intention of Parliament in creating the Act.

Literal Rule

Where judges give the words in the legislation their **"ordinary, natural" meaning**, as clearly stated in the Sussex Peerage case in 1844 **and as such upholds the separation of powers doctrine – judges clearly interpreting not making law.**
The problem is this rule can lead to absurd or unjust results, as seen in the following cases:

Whitley v Chappel (1868)   A statute aimed at preventing electoral malpractice was made a nonsense of when the accused was found not guilty of the offence when he impersonated a dead person, to use his vote. The court held, using the literal rule, a **dead person was not "entitled to vote".**

LNER v Berriman (1946)   The widow of a railway worker killed at work, was denied compensation due to the interpretation of the Fatal Accidents Act. It was held that the worker who was **maintaining and oiling** the track when he was killed, **did not fall within the literal meaning of "relaying or repairing"** in the Act. This caused an injustice where Parliament probably never intended any.

Fisher v Bell(1961)   Is another example of an absurd result. Here, the intention of Parliament (to reduce the number of offensive weapons available, including flick knives) was rendered ineffective by the literal rule of interpretation when it was held that **placing flick knives on display in a shop window did not fall within the contract law meaning of "offering for sale"** stated within the Act. The defendant was therefore found not guilty. [however, Parliament subsequently changed the wording of the Act to prevent this occurring in future]

The judges did not have to use this rule, but chose to in order to be seen to be applying the law – as seen in the **dicta of Lord Esher** in

R v Judge of City of London (1892:
"If the words of an Act are clear, you must follow them, even though they lead to a manifest absurdity … the court has nothing to do with the question of whether the legislature has committed an   absurdity."

Law Commission, 1969 stated that the literal rule "assumes unattainable perfection in draftsmanship"
M Zander: "mechanical and divorced from both realities of the use of language and from the expectations of human beings concerned … in that sense it is irresponsible."

Golden Rule   If the literal rule creates an absurd or unjust result:
Modify the ordinary, natural meaning   OR   choose between different meanings

Narrow interpretation of this rule:
R v Allen (1872) – the words "shall marry" were interpreted to mean "shall go through a marriage ceremony". The court chose between possible meanings using the Golden rule. If the literal rule had been used the absurd result would have been that the offence of bigamy could not be committed!

Wider interpretation of this rule:
Maddox v Storer (1963) – minibus MADE to carry 11 passengers being held **"suitable for"** 11 passengers and not just literally **"adapted to".**

Adler v George (1964) Here the meaning of the words **"in the vicinity of"** in the Official Secrets Act 1920 was modified to mean **"within"** - in the context of the Act as a whole, in order to avoid an absurdity of the literal rule. Golden rule enabled verdict of guilty for obstruction of a member of the armed forces **on** an air force base.

Re Sigsworth (1935) – where the meaning of **"issue"** was modified on the grounds of public policy. The court were effectively writing into the Act "issue" would not be entitled to inherit where they had killed the deceased.

- The cases of wider interpretation show that the golden rule is often seen as the mischief rule in disguise – finding and upholding Parliaments intention in creating the Act, rather than merely applying a modified meaning of the ordinary, natural meaning of the words used in the Act. However, in using the Golden rule they are still seen to be applying law – upholding the doctrine of separation of powers.
- The Golden Rule has been **criticised by the Law Commission (in 1969)** as the rule provides **no clear meaning of an "absurd result", of when the rule can be used.**

Mischief Rule

interpret the words in the statute in the light of the ___gap / mischief___ in the law which Parliament intended to remedy. [i.e. interpret in way to give effect to "mischief" intended to remedy]

- This rule is purported to be used if the literal and golden rules produce an absurd or silly result.
- The golden and literal rules are concerned with finding out what Parliament said, whereas the Mischief rule looks for what Parliament tried to achieve (the "mischief" intended to remedy).
- **An old rule based on Heydon's case in 1584**. This approach lost favour in the strict Victorian times, and then regained favour as the **need for flexibility** was again recognised.

As seen in:

Smith v Hughes (1960) in this case a prostitute was calling **from the balcony** of a private house to men in the street below. If the offence to solicit **"in a street"** was interpreted literally the defendant would have been found not guilty. The court interpreted this phrase in the light of the Act's **clear intention to allow men to walk freely down the street without proposition** – finding the prostitute's actions to fall within this "mischief" Parliament intended to stop; hence to be guilty of the offence -using the mischief rule.

Royal College of Nursing v DHSS (1981) HL The controversial case in which Lord Wilberforce dissented claiming the House of Lords was not interpreting but was rewriting legislation. In the case the House looked to the mischief that the Act sought to remedy – namely the uncertain state of the previous law on abortions by **widening the grounds upon which legal abortions could be obtained and hygienically and safely so**. Literally interpreted, a nurse is not a "registered medical practitioner" hence would be guilty of carrying out an illegal abortion. However, was found to be within the Act using the mischief rule.

This Mischief Rule **helps avoid absurdity and injustice - o**vercomes problems with literal and golden rules. **It allows flexibility for the judge,** and has been described by the **Law Commission** in 1969 as *"a rather more satisfactory approach than the other established rules."* The **major criticism is that it contradicts the legal doctrine of separation of powers** as judges are re-writing the Act – **making law.**

The Purposive Approach

Has been **inherited from EC law, and described as a modern descendant of the mischief rule**. This rule is where judges look at the purpose of the legislation and **interpret the words to bring about that purpose.**

- **An approach which Lord Denning was in favour of** when interpreting all legislation, as seen in his dicta in Magor and St Mellons v Newport Corporation **(1950)** *"We sit here to find out the intention of Parliament and carry it out, and we do this better by filling in the gaps and making sense of the enactment than by opening it up to destructive analysis."* A broader approach than the mischief rule.
- **However, at the time Lord Denning's approach was criticised by the House of Lords**: Lord Simonds described Lord Denning's approach as *"a naked usurpation of the legislative function under the thin disguise of interpretation."* Further *"if a gap is disclosed the remedy lies in an amending Act"*
- **Since 1972, England's entry into the European Union, English judges have been interpreting EC law purposively in English courts**. *[All EC law is interpreted purposively. The literal rule would be inappropriate due to the problem of meaning lost in the translation of words in the different member states of the European Union.]*
- **As the judges become more used to using this approach when interpreting EC law, so they may apply it more willingly when interpreting English legislation**. This is seen in House of Lords case *Maunsel v Olins (1975)* where Lord Simon stated that judges should endeavour to interpret Parliament's words to bring about the effect that was intended.
- **The introduction of the Human Rights Act 1998 is likely to prompt a shift towards more purposive interpretation** as judges take account of the European Court of Human Rights; which itself takes a purposive approach to interpretation.
- **Main criticism: how to accurately find intention of Parliament / judges making law.**

Approach	*advantages*	*disadvantages*
Literal rule	**judges apply law**	**can lead to unjust / absurd results**
Golden rule	**judges apply law** and yet avoid unjust / absurd result of literal rule	cannot always be applied: not always able to modify ordinary meaning of word: is often mischief rule in disguise. No clear meaning of "absurd result".

literal and golden rules uphold doctrines of Parliamentary supremacy / separation of powers

Mischief rule and **Purposive**	**provide just / result** - avoid unjust / absurd result of the Literal & Golden rules **Promotes flexibility.**	argued not easy to accurately find "mischief / gap" parliament intended to remedy – nor to accurately find Parliament's intention. **judges making law.**

Mischief and Purposive do NOT strictly uphold the doctrine of separation of powers

It is the **judge's discretion which rule to use**, which **can lead to different results** depending upon the approach used. **This in turn leaves the English legal system with an element of uncertainty and inconsistency**.

Aids - to interpretation

Whichever approach the judge takes to interpreting the legislation, he will have at his disposal **a range of material AIDS to help find** the exact **meaning of the words** / phrases in the legislation **OR   Parliament's intention** -   the "mischief" which Parliament intended to remedy.

> Aids: **Intrinsic   [internal]   connected with the Act**
> **Extrinsic   [external]   outside the Act**

For EC law the judge can make an Article 234 referral to ECJ for clarification of meaning (and validity) of piece of EC law. [see page 33]

For Literal and Golden rules To find **meaning of words**	**For Mischief and Purposive** To find **gap in law / intention** of Parliament
INTERNAL:	INTERNAL:
Definition sections within the Act [Presumptions] **Rules of language**	Long and short **title** in the Act [Presumptions] **Preamble**
EXTERNAL:	EXTERNAL:
Dictionary Textbook Earlier case law	Historical setting **Hansard** Earlier case law **Royal Commission reports**

The Interpretation Act 1978
Is an aid to interpretation: rule that singular includes plural / "he" includes "she"
Royal Commission reports / official reports
In 1975, the House of Lords declared that such reports can be used as external aids to find the "mischief" that Parliament intends to remedy – in the case of Black-Clawson International Ltd (1975).

Hansard

Hansard is **the official record of parliamentary debates.**

In 1993, the **House of Lords declared that Hansard could be used as an external aid for the mischief / purposive approach –** in **Pepper v Hart (1993).** [This case is also an example of the House of Lords using the practice statement to overrule their own previous decision banning the use of Hansard – see page 21]

However, House of Lords only allowed use of Hansard in limited way:
To clarify ambiguous words/phrases in an Act:
- o **Only where words of the Act are ambiguous or obscure or lead to an absurdity**
- o **And only if there was a clear statement by the Minister introducing the legislation**
[objection to overuse being time and cost to research Hansard in every case]

A wider use of Hansard is permitted when judges are interpreting Act or delegated legislation introduced in order to give effect to EC law or international convention – as held in Three Rivers District Council and others v Bank of England (No2) (1996). **Here Hansard was used to find the purpose of the legislation** / intention in enacting.

The House of Lords have since re-iterated the limited use, and emphasising its use to clarify ambiguity over meaning and intended aim of social policy of the Act – in Wilson v Secretary of State for Trade and Industry (2003).

Arguments for using Hansard:

Useful aid:
As per Lord Denning: to ignore Hansard would be to *"grope in the dark for the meaning of an Act without switching on the light"*.

Many foreign jurisdictions use such legislative materials as aids to interpretation.

Media: Parliamentary debates are reported in the media – judges aware so why not be used in court?

Arguments against using Hansard:

Lack of clarity: debates do not necessarily clarify the meaning/intention of legislation – even the speech by minister introducing the legislation.
Not always helpful: court could have reached same conclusion without using Hansard: as per study by Vera Sachs in 1982.
Time & Expense: concern that lawyers would spend too much time / cost considering Hansard

Since 1993, Hansard has been used in a number of cases – along with <u>increasing use of purposive approach</u> to statutory interpretation by judges.

Presumptions:

Unless the Act in question clearly states otherwise, **the courts will assume**:

- **Statutes do not alter common law -** common law will apply
- **Mens rea is required in crime -** must have required mental element (e.g. intention)
- **legislation not apply retrospectively -** Act applies from date it comes into effect, not to past happenings
- **The Crown is not bound**

Rules of language:

Internal aids to interpreting statutes
used with **Literal** and **Golden** principles

Developed by judges over time, these rules reflect the common sense approach to look at words in a sentence in the light of other words in the Act.

Ejusdem generis

LIST + general words

general words are limited to kind of items in the list

e.g.
house, barn (specific words) and other such similar places (general words)
e.g.
"cats, dogs and other such animals". Under this rule the other animals must be of the same kind as "cats, dogs", arguably domestic animals / pets.

As seen in:
Powell v Kempton Park Racecourse (1899) "house, office, room or other place for betting" **Held outdoor tent called "Tattersall's Ring" did not fall within meaning of words in the Act as it was outdoors, and the specific words in the Act were limited to indoor places.** Hence defendant not guilty of offence.

There must be at least 2 specific words in order to create a list – *Allen v Emerson (1944)*

Expressio Unius

LIST (all specific words) + NO general words

Express mention of one thing implies the exclusion of another

e.g. if Act specifically mentioned "Persian cats and Siamese cats" (and no general words) then under this rule the Act would not apply to other breeds of cat.
As seen in:
Tempest v Kilner (1846) – whether "goods, wares and Merchandise" listed in Statute of Frauds 1677 applied to sale of stocks and shares. Held that **stocks and shares were not in the list** [and there were no general words] **hence sale of stocks and shares not have to comply with requirements of the Act**: i.e. sale not need to
be evidenced in writing.

Noscitur a sociis
NOT USUALLY A LIST

a word is known by the company it keeps

look at words **in context of Act as a whole, and interpret accordingly**
[look at words in same section or in other sections]
e.g.
If an Act states "hamster cages, straw and food", the meaning of "food" is found by looking at the other words in the sentence – hence meaning hamster food and not dog food.
As seen in:
Inland Revenue Commissioners v Frere (1965)) – **"other annual interest" stated in the same section of the Act led the court to declare that "interest" only meant annual interest.**
Bromley LBC v GLC (1982) concerned the operation of a cheap fare scheme which resulted in the GLC running at a loss. **The court held that "economic" meant run on business lines by looking at another section in the Act which detailed a duty to make up any deficit. Hence held the cheap fares policy to be illegal.**

Exam Question on Statutory Interpretation:

1   (a)   Describe three internal or intrinsic aids available to the judge to assist in the process of statutory interpretation.

       (b)   The Source, at lines 10-12, refers to the rules of language.
Consider all three rules and explain (using cases to illustrate) which rule is likely to be applied to each situation:

            (iii)   An Act uses the phrase 'hamsters, dogs, cats and other animals' and the animal in question is a tiger;

            (ii)   An Act states that it specifically applies to 'hamsters, dogs and cats' and animal in question is a tiger;

            (iii)   An Act mentions 'tigers, cages and food' and the 'food' in question is domestic cat food.

       (c)   With reference to the Source:

            (i)   Briefly describe and illustrate both the literal and the purposive approach.

            (ii)   Discuss the advantages and disadvantages of the purposive approach.

OCR AS Level Law, January 2005, Q2

<u>New specification specimen question</u>:   [see page 11 for example of a question]

Question with 3 parts: a, b, c,
which must be answered <u>with reference to the source</u> (printed material) provided – total of 60 marks.

       (a)   12 marks … AO1 … **"describe, explain"**   e.g. approaches &/or aids…

       (b)   15 marks … AO2 … **3 problem scenarios to apply law to.**

       (c)   27 marks in total, split as follows:

          c   (i)   15 marks – AO1 - "describe"; &
          c   (ii)   12 marks – AO2   - " discuss, comment upon …"

     [6 marks for AO3 which is global for the paper]
      a total of 60 raw marks   [40% of total AS Law marks]

Statutory interpretation may be examined on its own, or along with law reform or EC law or legislation / delegated legislation.

o *You need to know:*
- o What judicial precedent is
- o How judges apply this doctrine
- o Different methods of flexibility of application of the doctrine
  - ▪ E.g. distinguishing / Practice Statement / Young's case exceptions
  - ▪ Plus able to explain overruling a decision.

o *Need to be able to comment upon:*
- o Advantages and disadvantages of rigid application of the doctrine.
- o When the House of Lords have used the Practice Statement
  - o Link with: separation of powers doctrine / do judges make law – should they?
- o When the Court of Appeal can use the exceptions created in Young's case
- o Lord Denning's challenges to the application of this doctrine.
- o **Link with topics of legislation, delegated legislation, law reform and EC law.**

* *

The Hallmark of any good decision making process is consistency in cases [like cases should be treated alike], **which leads to certainty in law.**   In our English legal system this is **provided by the rigid application of the <u>legal doctrine</u> of Judicial Precedent.**

Judicial Precedent: enables judges decisions to become law
- • Is a judicially created legal doctrine
- • Based upon Latin maxim: **stare decisis** (let decision stand)

- • Which states that:

  - o **inferior courts must follow earlier decisions of higher or same level courts, in cases of similar material facts.**

- • It is the **ratio decidendi – legal reason for the decision** – which can form **binding precedent** to be followed by lower or same level courts, in future cases of similar facts. The Obiter Dicta is anything else said in the judgment – this forms **persuasive precedent** – may follow if wish.

- • **This doctrine is RIGIDLY APPLIED:**
  Judges **must follow (apply)** a binding previous ratio decidendi, in cases of similar material facts, - when previous case decided in same level or higher court – **whether they like it or not** – i.e. whether it gives a just and fair outcome to the case before them, or not.
  - o The **advantage** of this rigid application is that it leads to **consistency in cases** and hence to **certainty in law**
  - o The **disadvantage** is that it does **not always enable a fair and just outcome in the current case – nor does it enable law to evolve** [law should evolve in line with the changing social and economic climate]

In order to overcome these disadvantages the judges have created **situations where they can be FLEXIBLE IN THEIR APPLICATION** of this doctrine:
- ➢ **situations where they do not have to follow a binding previous precedent (ratio)**
- ➢ situations where judges can achieve a fair and just result in the current case - correct errors in previous decisions - and enable law to evolve.
  - ▪ All judges can **distinguish** material facts
  - ▪ House of Lords can use **Practice Statement**, since 1966
  - ▪ Court of Appeal has **exceptions stated in Young's case**, since 1944

However, with this flexibility comes inconsistency in cases, and uncertainty in law.
Hence the judges display a reluctance / cautiousness when using this flexibility.

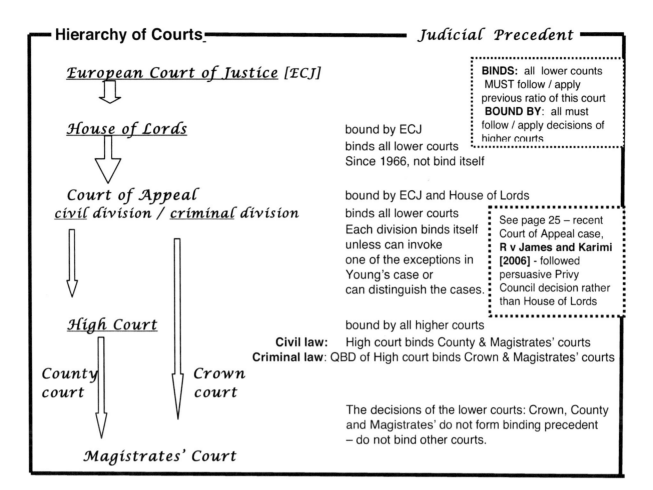

Hierarchy of Courts — Judicial Precedent

European Court of Justice [ECJ]

House of Lords
bound by ECJ
binds all lower courts
Since 1966, not bind itself

BINDS: all lower counts MUST follow / apply previous ratio of this court
BOUND BY: all must follow / apply decisions of higher courts

Court of Appeal
civil division / *criminal* division
bound by ECJ and House of Lords
binds all lower courts
Each division binds itself
unless can invoke
one of the exceptions in
Young's case or
can distinguish the cases.

See page 25 – recent Court of Appeal case, **R v James and Karimi [2006]** - followed persuasive Privy Council decision rather than House of Lords

High Court
bound by all higher courts
Civil law: High court binds County & Magistrates' courts
Criminal law: QBD of High court binds Crown & Magistrates' courts

County court

Crown court

The decisions of the lower courts: Crown, County and Magistrates' do not form binding precedent – do not bind other courts.

Magistrates' Court

FLEXIBILITY: when courts do not have to follow a binding precedent (previous case ratio)
In ALL COURTS: Judge can apply **DISTINGUISHING**
In HOUSE OF LORDS: Since **1966**, the judge can use **Practice Statement** to not follow **previous House of Lords decision.** (or can use distinguishing)
In COURT OF APPEAL: Since **1944**, the judge does not have to follow a **previous Court of Appeal decision** in certain situations - as stated in the case of **Young v Bristol Aeroplane Co Ltd** (1944). (can also distinguish other previous decisions)

DISTINGUISHING

The doctrine of Judicial Precedent does not come into play if the previous case and the current case do not have similar material facts. Therefore, **different material facts mean a judge in any court can distinguish between the current and previous precedent case and not have to follow what seems to be a previous binding precedent.**

As seen in:

Merritt v Merritt (1971) where husband and wife were separated when they made an agreement that the husband would pay maintenance to the wife. A similar agreement was reached in the case of *Balfour v Balfour (1919)*, where it was held such an agreement was not legally enforceable (merely a casual arrangement between husband and wife).

The **material difference** between the two cases was the circumstances of the parties when the agreement was made: still living together in Balfour case but separated in Merritt case (also several steps taken which indicated parties intention to create a legally binding agreement). These differences in material facts enabled the judge in *Merritt v Merritt* to reach a different outcome : to declare that the agreement was legally binding / legally enforceable. The judge in Merritt did not follow the ratio of Balfour – **declaring he distinguished the two cases, allowing the judge to reach a different decision in Merritt case.**

Some judges are more inclined than others to distinguish to avoid decisions they feel are outdated or "wrong":

Lord Reid:
"It is notorious that where an existing decision is disapproved but cannot be overruled courts tend to distinguish it on inadequate grounds… adopting the less bad of the only alternatives open to them. But this is bound to lead to uncertainty."

20

> Original position: House of Lords bound itself - bound by its own previous decisions, as stated in ***London Street Tramways v London County Council in 1898 – that as the highest appeal court their decisions should be final.***   This is **to achieve certainty in law**; which the House of Lords stated was **more important than the possibility hardship in individual cases being caused through having to follow a previous decision.**

Recognising the need for the law to adapt to reflect social and economic change; and the judges role in such development – the Lord Chancellor [Lord Gardiner] issued the **Practice Statement in 1966:**   which enables judges in the House of Lords to **depart** from their **own previous binding decision "when it appears right to do so"**

DISCRETIONARY – up to House of Lords when to use this Practice Statement. The effect of the Practice Statement is to **overrule** the previous decision : the ratio decidendi is no longer valid law to be followed by lower courts – but the outcome in the case remains the same for the parties involved. The current case ratio becomes the "new law" – binding precedent.

At first the House of Lords displayed a **reluctance** to use the Practice statement:

> Issued in 1966 but not used until 1968
> And then merely to alter a technical point concerning discovery of documents in the case of ***Conway v Rimmer (1968).***
> Displaying a reluctance to override certainty in law and to be seen to be making law.

REASONS FOR HOUSE OF LORDS USING THE PRACTICE STATEMENT:

To *reflect change* in **social conditions** in society: to develop the law

> **First major use of the Practice Statement was in 1972**
> ***British Railways Board v Herrington (1972)*** when they altered the test for the duty of care (in tort) owed to child trespassers to reflect change in social and physical conditions. A test of 'common humanity' – doing all that a humane person would have done to protect the safety of the child trespasser thus **overruling their previous decision in *Addie v Dumbreck (1920)*** which held the test was that of injuries caused 'intentionally or recklessly'.
> **In the same year, still stated a reluctance to use the Practice Statement:**
> As seen in ***Jones v Secretary of State for Social Services (1972)*** where despite 4 out of the 7 Lords agreeing that the previous decision in Re Dowling (1967) was wrong, they decided not to overrule the decision in order to retain certainty in case law.

To *reflect change* in **economic climate:** to develop the law

> In ***Miliangos v George Frank (Textiles)*** Ltd in 1976, the Lords **recognised the change in stability of sterling** since the previous ruling in 1961 in ***Re United Railways of Havana and Regla Warehouses*** where they had held that damages could only be paid in sterling.

To correct errors / restore certainty:

> In ***Murphy v Brentwood District Council (1990)*** the Lords overruled their previous decision in ***Anns v Merton District Council (1977)*** in order **to correct the stated test for negligence in the law of Tort**.

To develop the law:

> ***In Pepper v Hart (1993)*** the Lords **overruled their previous ban on the use of Hansard as an external aid to statutory interpretation**. Enabling greater use of external aids to find "mischief" / intention of Parliament in creating legislation – as greater use of purposive approach to statutory interpretation is being seen. [see page 14].

When considering use of the Practice Statement the Lords are balancing the need for certainty in law, with the need for justice in the case before them.

Criminal Law:

The Practice Statement itself states the **"especial need for certainty in criminal law"**
However, the Lords have overruled their own previous decisions in criminal law:

> **1st use in criminal case was in *R v Shivpuri (1986)*** [20 years after practice statement was introduced] where Lords overruled their previous decision in *Anderton v Ryan (1985)* – made only a year earlier – **to correct their previous misinterpretation of a statute** and stop further perpetuation of their error by lower courts.
>
> In *R v R and G (2003)* the Lords overruled their previous decision in *R v Caldwell (1982),* **altering the definition of recklessness in criminal law** back to that of a subjective test of the defendant realising a risk of damage and taking the risk.

The above cases show that the House of Lords, from the mid 70's, has shown a greater willingness to use the Practice Statement, and overrule their own previous decision.
It seems that they are willing to use this power in order to:
 ➢ **Correct their own previous errors; and**
 ➢ **To develop the law in line with changing social and economic climate**
[Alan Paterson carried out a survey on when and why the House of Lords used the Practice Statement between 1967 and 1973. He concluded that 12 out of 19 Law Lords felt they had a duty to develop the common law in response to changing social conditions.]

The House of Lords, whilst recognising that judges do make law, are mindful of the constitutional issue *that certain areas are best suited for Parliament to legislate upon:*

> In *C v DPP (1995)* the House of Lords considered the common law presumption of doli incapax was outdated and produced some absurd results. However they did not use the Practice Statement to abolish this presumption, instead stating that **it was for Parliament to review and legislate**.
> [Presumption that a child of between 10 & 14 years old <u>can only be prosecuted with proof that the child knew their actions were seriously wrong</u> – altered by Parliament in the Crime and Disorder Act 1998]
>
> This case can be contrasted with the case of *R v R (1991)* where the House of Lords **held that a husband could be criminally liable for raping his wife**. This decision abolished the 250 year old immunity for husbands. Lord Keith stated that their decision to overrule the previous law was in order **to develop the law in the light of changing social and cultural developments**.

However, sometimes the House of Lords has no option but to create new law – original precedent: they have to make a decision in the case.

> In *Re S (1992)* the House of Lords had to decide whether to grant a health authority the legal right to carry out an emergency **Caesarean** to save the life of the patient and of her baby, **despite the patient's refusal of such treatment**, on religious grounds. The Lords granted the declaration sought, acknowledging that there was no English legal authority on this issue.
>
> Another controversial case was that of *Gillick v W. Norfolk Area Health Authority (1995)* where the House of Lords held by a majority that a girl under sixteen did not have to have parental consent to receive **contraceptive services,** provided she was mature enough to make up her own mind.
> In such cases the judges have no option but to made a decision, albeit reluctant to create new law on such issues. In *Airdale NHS Trust v Bland (1993)* the House of Lords stated the judges' role is *"to apply the principles which society, through the democratic process, adopts, not to impose their standards on society."*

> **Original precedent** is where the judge has to make a decision in the case before him and yet finds there is no previous case law to consider – and often no guidance in legislation. Here the judge is making law, which can form binding precedent for future cases.

Young's case exceptions

The Court of Appeal:

The two divisions of the Court of Appeal (Civil & Criminal) do not bind each other – do not have to follow each other's previous decisions; but **each division does bind itself.**

In 1944, the Court of Appeal created exceptions to this rule:

3 exceptions for the civil division, and 4 exceptions for the criminal division, were created in the case of *Young v Bristol Aeroplane Co Ltd (1944): [Young's case]*
situations where the Court of Appeal does not have to follow its own previous decisions:

1   previous decision was made *per incuriam*
2   **since** previous decision the **House of Lords have given a conflicting decision**
3   **There are two or more conflicting** Court of Appeal previous decisions

And for criminal cases:
4. where law was "misapplied or misunderstood" in previous decision.

In 2001, a fourth exception was created for the civil division:
R Kadham v Brent London Borough Housing Benefit Review Board (2001)
A proposition of law which was not considered in the previous decision, but assumed to exist.

Per Incuriam   This rule can be used in situations where the previous Court of Appeal case was decided: [as stated by Lord Evershed in *Morelle v Wakeling (1955)*]
a)   **in ignorance of a relevant law [legislation or common law]; and**
b)   **that ignorance led to faulty reasoning**

That is, that there was a major oversight in reaching the decision; not simply that the court previously reached the wrong decision; **and today, only when the court would have reached a different decision had the relevant law been applied.**   This exception enables the Court of Appeal the flexibility not to follow their own previous decision, and possibly to create a new law.

The Court of Appeal do use this exception, as seen in:

In *Wiliams v Fawcett (1986)* – the Court of Appeal refused to follow their own previous decision, declaring that it had been **based on a misunderstanding of County Court rules.** –*per incuriam.*
In *Rickards v Rickards (1989)* the Court of Appeal refused to follow their own previous decision declaring that it had **misunderstood the effect of a House of Lords decision.** – *per incuriam.*

Conflicting decision from House of Lords:

The previous Court of Appeal decision was not appealed up to the House of Lords, however in a different case the House of Lords have since made a ruling which conflicts with the previous Court of Appeal decision. [**impliedly overruled**]   **Under the rules of judicial precedent the Court of Appeal follow the binding precedent of the House of Lords.**

Conflicting previous Court of Appeal decisions:

The Court of Appeal can **choose which of their own previous decisions to follow.**
As seen in *Starmark Enterprises Ltd v CPL Distribution Ltd (2001)* where the Court of Appeal chose to follow the earlier of the two previous conflicting Court of Appeal decisions, in the current case concerning a rent review clause in a lease of property.

"Missaplied or misunderstood"

This exception is wider than the rule on per incuriam, in recognition that in criminal law a person's liberty is involved .

As stated in *R v Spencer (1985)* "… *if departure from authority is necessary in the interests of justice to an appellant, then this court should not shrink from so acting.*"

This further exception was used in *R v Taylor (1950)* and in *R v Gould (1968)* enabling the Court of Appeal to refuse to follow their own previous decision and reach a "just" decision.

The Court of Appeal :
- **Is bound by decisions of the House of Lords**   [see R v James and Karimi (2006) on page 25]
- **Can only depart from its own previous decisions in certain situations** [see page -23]

[unless they can distinguish between the previous and current cases]

> Lord Denning argued that:
> - the Court of Appeal was in essence the final court of appeal for many cases.
> - As such, it **should have the same flexibility in the doctrine of judicial precedent as the House of Lords:**
> - greater flexibility with regard to its own previous decisions;
> - and not to be bound by House of Lords decisions where the law needed to evolve, or their decision was *per incuriam.*

Challenge to the rule in Young's case:

Lord Denning declared his view in the case of ***Gallie v Lee (1969),*** stating that the Court of Appeal needed greater flexibility than the limited exceptions they gave themselves in Young's case – stating a need to be able to depart from their own previous decisions "when it is right to do so" as the House of Lords can since the Practice Statement. Lord Denning argued that Young's case exceptions are
" *a self-imposed limitation and we who imposed it can also remove it."*

Russell, LJ, did not agree: "*the availability of the House of Lords to correct errors in the Court of Appeal makes it, in my view, unnecessary for the court to depart from its existing discipline."*

The challenge can be seen in the case of *Davis v Johnson (1979)* where Court of Appeal, under Lord Denning's leadership, **refused to follow its own previous decision** concerning their interpretation of the Domestic Violence and Matrimonial Proceedings Act 1996 – **without distinguishing or invoking a Young's case exception.**   On appeal, **the House of Lords declared that although they agreed with the Court of Appeal's interpretation, they "*expressly, unequivocally and unanimously reaffirmed the rule in Young v Bristol Aeroplane"*** – clearly stating that the Court of Appeal are restricted to their current exceptions.

Challenge to the rule that Court of Appeal are bound by House of Lords decisions :

Lord Denning believed the role of a judge is to enable the law to evolve to reflect the changing conditions of society; and to ensure justice in the case before them. Believing that the decision in ***Rooks v Barnard (1964),*** of the House of Lords was made *per incuriam (*as it failed to consider its own previous authority with regard to when exemplary damages can be awarded); **The Court of Appeal refused to follow the earlier House of Lords decision in the similar case of *Broome v Cassell (1971).***   On appeal, the House of Lords rebuked Lord Denning and declared that under the doctrine of judicial precedent it is necessary for all lower courts *"including the Court of Appeal, to accept loyally the decisions of the higher tiers"* – Lord Hailsham.
The House of Lords did then use the Practice Statement to ovverule their previous decision in *Rooks v Barnard* agreeing with Lord Denning that it should be altered, but stating it was not his place to do so.

Further challenges were made in the cases of ***Schorsch* Meier GmbH v Henning (1975)** and ***Miliangos* v George Frank (Textiles) Ltd (1976).** These both concerned the previous House of Lords decision in the *Havana Railways case*, which held that damages could only be awarded in pounds sterling. [see page 21].   Lord Denning felt the economic climate had changed - that sterling was no longer such a strong and stable currency. Damages were awarded in other currencies in both cases before the Court of Appeal.

Only the Miliangos case was appealed to the House of Lords; who emphatically **reiterated their statement made in *Broome v Cassell* (above) declaring that the Court of Appeal has no right to ignore or overrule HL decisions. Again the House of Lords did then use the Practice Statement to ovverule their previous decision in the *Havana Railways* case** - agreeing with Lord Denning that it should be altered, but stating that it was not for the Court of Appeal to do so.

> *Schorsch case highlights the problem outlined by Lord Denning: that not all cases are appealed for House of Lords to overrule an outdated or "wrong" previous legal reasoning.*

o **Overruling**

The ratio decidendi of the previous case is no longer law.

but does **not alter the outcome** for the previous case – [merely creates new precedent.]

e.g.   When the House of Lords use the Practice Statement to overrule their own previous decisions and create a new binding ratio (legal reasoning)

Examples of persuasive precedent:
- ➤ Ratio of lower court
- ➤ Obiter of dissenting judgment
- ➤ Obiter of higher court
- ➤ Decisions of Privy Council

Persuasive precedents are those decisions which are not binding on a court but which may be applied. However, the **Court of Appeal in *R v James and Karimi (2006)*** applied a previous Privy Council decision [AG for Jersey v Holley (2005], effectively overruling the previous House of Lords decision in Smith (Morgan) (2001), concerning the test for provocation, as a partial defence to murder. The Court of Appeal acknowledged that this went against the established rules of judicial precedent – explaining this was an exceptional case in which those rules should not apply.

---

o **Reversing**

alters the outcome of the previous case **and** the legal reasoning (precedent) is that of the new case – alters outcome and law.

e.g.   When a decision of a lower court is appealed to a higher court. The higher court may reverse (overturn) the decision of the lower court in the case – altering the outcome of that case for the parties involved.

Judges do make law:

Through the doctrine of judicial precedent, judges are continually applying the existing rules to new fact situations, often creating new laws.

As Lord Radcliffe has stated *"… there was never a more sterile controversy than that upon the question of whether a judge makes law. Of course he does. How can he help it?"* ['Not in Feather Beds', 1968]

In this respect the doctrine of separation of powers is not strictly applied – however, **judges still recognise the constitutional point that Parliament is the main legislator in our English legal system.** As stated by Lord Brandon, to make new law where there is reason to believe that Parliament does not support such changes is *"an unjustifiable usurpation of the function which properly belongs to Parliament."* However, [as seen above, p22] judges may find they have no choice but to create law in order to resolve the case before them – **original precedent.** Further, the use of the practice statement and the Young's case exceptions supports the view that **judges are no longer merely 'declaring' the existing law under the doctrine of judicial precedent.**

ADVANTAGES of Judicial Precedent

- ➤ **Rigid application provides**:
  - ❖ **Uniformity in law** through consistency in cases [like cases treated alike]
  - ❖ **Certainty in law** through being able to predict which decision will be applied.
  - ❖ Upholds doctrine of separation of power [judges applying law]
- ➤ **Flexible application provides:**
  - ❖ **Development of law** [in line with changing social and economic climate of society]
  - ❖ **[Although this is at the expense of consistency in cases and certainty in law.]**
- ➤ The doctrine is **practical in nature** – based on real facts, unlike legislation
- ➤ The doctrine **is detailed** – there are many cases to refer to.

DISADVANTAGES of Judicial Precedent

- o Depends upon a case coming to court
- o Difficulties can arise in finding the ratio in a judgment
- o Cases can be distinguished on their facts to avoid following an inconvenient precedent – if used too often (and there are cases where the distinguishing is somewhat spurious, as a means to avoid applying a previous legal reasoning) this creates uncertainty in law – and undermines the doctrine of judicial precedent.

Exam Question on Judicial Precedent:

1   (a)   *"ratio decidendi and obiter dicta"*.
            Describe and illustrate what is meant by **both** of these terms.

      (b)   *[There are various methods by which judges avoid having to apply past precedents.]*
            Explain which method of avoidance is **most** suited to each of the scenarios below. Illustrate your answer where appropriate:

          (i)   The House of Lords wish to depart from a past decision of their own;

          (ii)   on appeal, the Court of Appeal disagrees with a ruling of the High Court and wishes to replace it with a different decision;

          (iii)   A judge in the Crown Court does not wish to follow a past precedent of a higher court as she feels that the facts are slightly different.

      (c)   Discuss the advantages and disadvantages of having a system that requires judges to follow binding precedents.   *OCR AS Level Law, June 2005, Q2*

2   (a)   Describe how the method of distinguishing can be used to avoid having to apply a previous decision.

      (b)   In the case of *Herrington v British Railways Board (1972)* the House of Lords decided to overrule the decision that they had made years earlier in the case of *Addie v Dumbreck (1929)*.
            Consider how the doctrine of precedent would apply had the cases of Herrington v British Railsways Board and Addie v Dumbreck been heard in the following situations and on the following dates instead of when they were actually heard:

          (ii)   *Addie v Dumbreck* was decided by the House of Lords in 1950. *Herrington v British Railways Board* comes before the House of Lords in 1951;

          (ii)   *Addie v Dumbreck* was decided by the House of Lords in 1950. *Herrington v British Railways Board* comes before the House of Lords in 1967;

          (iii)   *Addie v Dumbreck.* was decided by the Court of Appeal (Civil Division) in 1950.   *Herrington v British Railways Board* comes before the Court of Appeal (Civil Division) in 2006.

      (c)   *[The Source refers to the need for certainty in the law …].*
            Using the Source and your knowledge of cases, discuss the House of Lords' use of the Practice Statement. [30]   *OCR AS Level Law, January 2006, Q2*

New specification specimen question: [see page 11 for example of a question]
Question with 3 parts: a, b, c, which must be answered <u>with reference to the source</u> (printed material) provided - total of 60 marks.
      (a)   12 marks … AO1 … "describe, explain"
      (b)   15 marks … AO2 … 3 problem scenarios to apply law to.
      (c)   27 marks in total, split as follows:
            c(i) 15 marks - AO1 -"describe"; & c(ii) 12 marks – AO2 - " discuss, comment upon"
[6 marks for AO3 which is global for the paper] A total of 60 raw marks [40% of total AS Law marks] *Judicial Precedent may be examined on its own, or along with law reform or EC law or legislation / delegated legislation.*

- o *You need to know:*
    - o *How* and *why* the law is reformed [altered / changed]
    - o *Who* influences Parliament to reform the law
    - o The bodies set up by Parliament specifically to look into law reform

- o *Need to be able to comment upon:*
    - o The Law Commission's role in law reform
    - o Those who influence Parliament
    - o In brief, the judicial role in law reform
    - o The advantages and disadvantages of the current system for law reform
    - o **Link with topics of legislation; delegated legislation; statutory interpretation; judicial precedent.**

* *

Law Reform concerns the concept of law as an instrument for **change**: to improve society and to reflect the changing social and economic climate of society.

The need for the law to change [be reformed] stems from the *function of law.* Today, law is not merely a set of rules created as a means of keeping the peace. The general function of *law* is to resolve conflict; regulate human behaviour; distribute power, wealth and property – to enable society to function and develop. As such **law should not remain static, but should evolve, in line with the changing and social economic climate of society.**

The topic of "Law Reform" in Sources of Law concerns the legal procedure for changing the law of our English legal system

---

Both the law and legal procedures cannot remain static

The law needs to under constant review, in order to:
- o **Repeal obsolete laws**
- o **Consolidate existing Acts** [for accessibility]
- o **Codify existing Acts and case law** [for accessibility]
- o **Eliminate anomalies**
- o **Create new law or develop existing law,** [in line with changing society]

Such review is carried out by:
- o **The Law Commission** – main reform body
- o **Committees** – for civil and for criminal law
- o **Ad Hoc committees** for particular areas of law

All of whom advise Parliament as to the necessary changes to the law – it is up to Parliament whether they enact those changes, or not. [Parliament reforms the law through legislation / delegated legislation]

Judges also develop the law, through the doctrine of judicial precedent, in the cases that come before them in the courts.

Influences upon Parliament to change the law:

- o From pressure groups / public opinion
- o To fulfil the government's election manifesto
- o From the judiciary declaring a need for reform in their judgments given in cases.

Bodies created specifically, by Parliament, to address need for law reform : *(to propose changes for Parliament to make)*

THE LAW COMMISSION = Main law reform (full-time)

Set up 1965 by Law Commission Act.
Function: S3 – to *"keep the law under review"*
Members: Chairman (High Court Judge), 4 Law Commissioners (from judiciary, legal profession & legal academics), plus support staff.

Role:
- **to systematically keep all law under review**
  (suggest proposals to simplify, repeal, consolidate, codify & develop existing law; create new law)
- both criminal and civil law, **on full time basis**
- areas of law as requested by **Lord Chancellor** – and own choice of projects.

Procedure:
- **researching** areas of law, **to identify** problem areas,**decide possible reform**
- publishing **consultation paper,** (to invite comments)
- drawing up **proposals for reform** – often with draft Bill
- **presenting proposals** to **Lord Chancellor** – who lays them before Parl.
- *It is up to the government whether or not to introduce the Bill into Parliament to enact the proposals* (make the proposals law)

Evaluate: looking at success rate:
- ➢ **85%** of proposals actually became law in **first ten years**
- ➢ **50%** of proposals actually became law **over next ten years**
- ➢ **No proposals became law in 1990**

The Law Commission website currently states that 174 law reform reports have been compiled since 1991; and that of these only 28 remain outstanding [15 of which have been accepted by the government but await debate.]

> **Lack of Parliamentary time to debate the proposals is the main reason for the lack of implementation of Law Commission proposals. This is even more noticeable in criminal law**. The draft Criminal Code proposal of 1995 has yet to be debated / enacted.
>
> * The increased power for government ministers to create or amend law to enact Law Commission recommendations is proposed in the **Legislative and Regulatory Reform Bill 2006** – [see page 10]
> * Arguably the creation of a separate **Ministry of Justice** department to support and pressure Parliament into enacting proposals., would also help to address the problem of lack of implementation of Law Commission Proposals.

> **Example of outdated laws:**
> - A scheme to provide farming work for ex-servicemen after the First World War had long fallen into disuse.
> - Victorian powers for the Metropolitan Police to license shoeblacks and commissionaires had become as irrelevant as the offence of fraudulently impersonating a shoeblack or commissionaire.
> - Lotteries to help struggling artists sell their work had become superseded by the modern law on lotteries.
>
> **All were repealed in The Statute Law (Repeals) Act 2004.**

examples of Acts enacting Law Commission proposals:-

Repeal : Criminal Law Act 1967 – following proposal to abolish certain ancient criminal offences
Statute Law Repeals Act - 17 have been enacted since 1995, repealing more than 2,000 whole Acts as well as partial repeal in thousands of other Acts.
Consolidation :
Rent Act 1977 – following proposal to combine several Acts concerning rent, into one Act
Powers of Criminal Courts (Sentencing) Act 2000 which consolidated the law on sentencing into one Act to improve accessibility.
[Note however, that there have since been alterations to the law on sentencing, the last being in the Criminal Justice Act 2003 – making the consolidating Act out of date today.]

Develop : Family Law Act 1996 - following proposal to developed the law on domestic violence and divorce,
Compute Misuse Act 1990 – following proposal to create new criminal offences regarding the misuse of computers.

example of current proposals for reform:
Consultation paper: "The Financial Consequences of Relationship Breakdown" CP170, published 31/05/06
[to develop the current law in line with change in society – increasing cohabitation of couples]

Bodies created specifically, by Parliament, to address need for law reform : (to propose changes for Parliament to make)

Law Reform Committee
- o Set up in 1952
- o **Part time**
- o **To propose reforms to civil law**
- o Small areas
- o As requested by Lord Chancellor
- o Often on technical points
- o **Members**: from the judiciary, legal profession and academic lawyers.

Proposals enacted:
Occupier's Liability Act 1957 [tort law]
Misrepresentation Act 1967 [contract law]
Civil Evidence Act 1968

Criminal Law Revision Committee
- o Set up in 1957
- o **Part time**
- o **To propose reforms to criminal law**
- o However, *last committee convened was in 1985*
- o **Members**: Director of Public Prosecutions, judges, legal profession and academic lawyers.
- o Responsible to Home Secretary

Proposed codification of law on theft – which was enacted in Theft Act 1968

Ad hoc committees:
- • Set up to consider one specific area of law for reform, then dissolved.
- • Usually chaired by a senior judge – but not all members are legally qualified.
- • Idea is that members are independent of the government, non-political.

➤ **Royal Commissions -**
- o Royal Commission **on Police Powers**, reported in 1981. Most proposals were enacted in PACE 1984, *(Police and Criminal Evidence Act 1984.)* *[Phillips Commission]*
- o Royal Commission **on Reform of the House of Lords**, reported in 2000 – the government accepted some of the proposals; but as yet these have not been enacted. *[Wakeham Commission]*

➤ **Judges may be asked to investigate a specific area**
- o Lord Woolf was asked, in 1996, to look into the **civil justice system**. Many of his proposals for reform were enacted in 1999. [see page 62]

ADVANTAGES of Law Reform

Law reform **enables the English legal system to evolve**: developing legal rules in line with changing social and economic climate in society; and developing legal procedure to create greater accessibility of the law.

➤ Reform in areas of high media / public pressure **helps to maintain public confidence in our legal system**. *"justice is seen to be done"* / *"Law for the people, by the people"*.

DISADVANTAGE :

Lack of implementation of Law Commission proposals
- o **Due to limited parliamentary time to debate and pass such Bills**. Those which are passed tend to be in response to strong public pressure, often in response to an event / incident; to "vote-catching" legislation. **Ultimately is up to government which proposals to enact:**
- o Political choice, by government, which become law - & whether to alter proposal
- o Judicial judgments continue to highlight the need for reform
- o **Creation of a Ministry of Justice Department**, responsible for law reform, could improve the lack of implementation – through prioritising and pressuring Parliament to debate / enact proposals.

Influence / Pressure is placed upon Parliament as to which areas of law to reform; by :-

Pressure groups

For example: Greenpeace / RSPCA / Bar Council / Charities / JUSTICE; **groups concerned with particular issues may press for reform in those areas using variety of tactics**: lobby MP's / protest / enlist media coverage.   Persistent pressure and media coverage help to persuade the government to respond by reforming the law.

o *Mary Whitehouse persistently campaigned for the government to legislate to prevent the growing instances of* **child pornography,** *which was addressed in the* **Children Act 1978.**

o *The enactment of the* **Disability Discrimination Act 1995,** *in response to pressure groups, created* **rights for disabled people** *with regard to access to shops and services, and in employment.*

Political parties

Some of the most high profile legislation passed is in order to implement government's election manifesto

o *The conservative government introduced the privatisation of gas and water; and the creation of the* **poll tax** *– as outlined in their election manifesto in the late 1970's.*

o *The Abortion Act 1967 started as a* **Private Members' Bill to legalise abortion.** [see page 2]

Civil Service

Each government department is headed by **a political minister; whose views as to the necessary legislation to achieve departmental goals influences Parliament**: e.g. re: reform of NHS / prisons

Public Opinion and Media Pressure

o **In response to events / incidents** *: the* **Dangerous Dogs Act** *was hurriedly enacted in response to pressure from the media following the* **incidents of pit- bull terriers attacking a man and a young girl** *– but proved to be rushed and unworkable.*

o *Media coverage highlighting the changes in society's attitude, and the public's wish for the law to reflect such changes, led to the* **Suicide Act 1961,** *and abolishing the prohibition on homosexuality in* **Sexual Offences Act 1967.**

Judiciary

When giving judgment in a case, judges may draw attention to the need for reform.

o In **R v Preddy (1996) and R v Graham and others (1996)** the **"gap" in the law** *enabling people who had committed mortgage fraud to be found not guilty*
was clearly highlighted as a need for reform which Parliament should address

o In **C v DPP (1995)** *the House of Lords considered the common law presumption of doli incapax was outdated and produced some absurd results. However they did not use the Practice Statement to abolish this presumption, instead* **stating that it was for Parliament to review and legislate.** *[Presumption that a child of between 10 & 14 years old can only be prosecuted with proof that the child knew their actions were seriously wrong – altered by Parliament in* **Crime and Disorder Act 1998***]*

Exam Question on Law Reform: This topic usually forms one of the three part questions on the Source paper question. As such, it is **usually linked with other source topics**: legislation & delegated legislation; judicial precedent; statutory interpretation or European law.

<u>The Law Reform part question is usually along the following lines:</u>

o asking you to **describe** the composition and role of the Law Commission

o asking you to **explain** the law reform bodies &/or other groups who influence Parliament to reform the law

o asking you to **comment upon** how effective such bodies (in b. above) are in persuading Parliament to reform the law.

o Asking you to **comment upon** how effective the Law Commission are in their role of law reform.

<u>New specification specimen question</u>:   [see page 11 for example of a question]
Question with 3 parts: a, b, c, which must be answered <u>with reference to the source</u> (printed material) provided - total of 60 marks.

a. 12 marks … AO1 … "describe, explain"

b. 15 marks … AO2 … 3 problem scenarios to apply law to.

c. 27 marks in total, split as follows: c (i) 15 marks – AO1 - "describe"; &
                              c (ii) 12 marks – AO2 - " discuss, comment upon"

[6 marks for AO3 which is global for the paper] total of 60 raw marks [**40% of total AS Law marks**]

European Law:

- ○ *You need to know:*
    - ○ The different European legal institutions: composition and role.
    - ○ The different types of European law
    - ○ The supremacy of European law
    - ○ An outline of the European Union

- ○ *Need to be able to comment upon:*
    - ○ Composition and role of European legal institutions
    - ○ The problems with directives – (enforceability)
    - ○ Supremacy of European law
        - ○ In relation to the sources of law in our English legal system
        - ○ Impact upon our parliamentary supremacy
    - ○ **Link with topics of legislation; delegated legislation; statutory interpretation; judicial precedent & law reform.**

* *

European Law as a source of law in our English legal system:
Because, **since 1973**, we have been a member of the European Union

---

The European Union [EU] is a new political and legal entity:
- ○ currently **25** countries within Europe (**member states**)
- ○ with a population of 460 million, it is culturally diverse, with 20 official languages
- ○ started in 1952 with 6 founding member states, who joined together with the aim of rebuilding Europe after WW1 & WW2 - & to prevent a further world war.
- ○ Based today upon the 3 pillars of:
- ○ European communities / Common Foreign & Security Policy / Police and Judicial Cooperation in criminal matters.

- ○ It is the **European Communities** pillar which concerns us, as this contains the legal framework ("constitution") for the European Union – its legal institutions and laws.
    - ○ Previously called European Economic Community
    - ○ **established by Treaty of Rome 1957**
- ○ *To achieve common goal of a free trade area*
- ○ Hence **based upon the legal principles in the Treaty : 4 freedoms**
    - • **Freedom of movement of : persons / capital / services / goods**
    - • **within the EU**
    - • The idea of no barriers to these 4 movements – a free trade area

- ○ **Today the EU is a political and legal entity which is constantly expanding and evolving in economic and political partnership between its member states**; with a clear and specific purpose : a single EU with unfettered free market competition.

<u>EU Institutions:</u>

Council	**Pass** [make] European Law (legislation)
Commission	**Propose** law
European Parliament	**Increasing legislative, but mainly supervisory role**
European Court of Justice [ECJ]	**Creates case law & general principles of law / resolves disputes**

<u>EU law</u> comes from:
Treaties
General principles created by ECJ
Case law of the ECJ (called "jurisprudence" of ECJ)
Legislation created by the institutions (regulations; directives; decisions; opinions)

> Most EU law is in the form of directives, which require the member states to make their objectives into national law in the member state. Hence, EU law is mainly implemented by the member states rather than the EU institutions.

COMMISSION - PROPOSE EC LAW

The "guardian of the Treaties"
The executive body of the EU - *The "motor" of the EU*
HQ Brussels

➢ consists of 30 Commissioners
➢ **1 from each member state** of the EU
   o (2 from some of the larger member states, including the UK)
➢ to form a body independent of the member states:
   o hence commissioners **represent interests of EU citizens,**
   o **not of their member state** *[unlike members of Council]*
➢ supported by an administrative body of European civil servants.

ROLE: [what they do]
Propose legislation
Guardian of the treaties: *(start infringement proceedings ECJ, against member states, EU institutions that it considers are in breach of EU law.)*
Negotiate international trade agreements **& Regulate competition within the EU.**
Note: The European Parliament must approve the entire Commission; and can force them all to resign – through a vote of no confidence.

COUNCIL   - PASS EC LAW   *[Regulations; Directives; Decisions; Opinions]*
Main legislative institution of the EU .HQ Brussels
➢ Presidency rotates amongst member states every 6 months.
➢ **1 representative (MP) from each member state,** chosen for each meeting according to the subject matter for discussion – e.g. farming / minister for agriculture.
➢ **Members represent national interest of their member state.**

ROLE: [what they do]

final say on **passing legislation; & *TO ENSURE:***
o **Treaty's objectives are obtained :** 4 freedoms
o **coordination of policies and decisions within EU**
   o Agree EU budget with European Parliament
   o Achieve common foreign; defence & economic policies common to all member states.
   o Seeks to coordinate the justice system of member states, especially with regard to terrorism.

> **ASSISTED BY:**
> o **Coreper:**
> Committee of permanent representatives (of member states) who set the Council agenda; negotiate minor, non-controversial matters.
> o **EU civil servants:**
> who offer general and legal advice and translation service.
> o **Economic & Social Committee :**
> who offer economic advice.

➢ Each member state is allocated a number votes depending on its size.
➢ A *qualified majority* is usually required to pass law.
   (voting is to be reformed in the proposed Treaty establishing a
   Constitution for Europe, 2004 – which has yet to become law / ratified by all member states)

➢ *In practice there are 9 different councils that meet in Brussels: each with concerned with a different policy area of the EU; each attended by ministers responsible for that area in their member state. However, legally, the Council is a single entity.*

➢ *Note: the Heads of government of the member states meet 4 times a year at the "European Summit" (called the "European Council") to discuss matters of policy concerning the EU.*

PARLIAMENT
The parliamentary body of the EU
Meets in Strasburg and Brussels

> ➢ consists of 732 MEPs
> *(members of European Parliament)*
> ➢ **Each member state sends MEPs which they elect every 5 years.**
> *(each member state is given seats approx. according to population.)*

ROLE:

Mainly supervisory role
- **over Commission:** can dismiss entire Commission / must approve Commission. Receives annual report from Commission.
- **over Council:** President of Council must address Parliament once a year.

Limited legislative role: can amend and block legislation in policy areas – other legislation may require Parliament to be consulted. However, unlike most national Parliaments, it cannot propose / make law.

Treaty establishing a European Constitution: *signed in 2004, but was rejected by French and Dutch voters in 2005. Other member states have since postponed ratification. The constitution will give the European Parliament greater legislative powers with regard to policy matters.*

EUROPEAN COURT OF JUSTICE:

Sits in Luxembourg
25 judges – 1 from each member state
- appointed under A222 of Treaty of Rome
- 11 sit in full court
- for 6 years. (can be re-appointed)

Assisted by 8 Advocate Generals
➢ Each case is assigned to an Advocate General who will compile a report of the legal issues raised in the case, along with their opinion for conclusions – for the judges to consider.
Judges & Advocate Generals are chosen from Those eligible for highest judicial posts in their own countries.

Differences between ECJ and courts in our English legal system:
- **Advocate Generals** giving persuasive decisions for judges to follow – not found in our system.
- **Only 1 judgment is delivered.** We record all judgments, including dissenting judgments (which do not agree with decision)
- **Judgment is brief**; but similarly it is often difficult to locate the ratio decidendi (legal reason for the decision)
- **Paper submission of cases** in contrast to the oral presentation of arguments in our courts.
- **No system of judicial precedent.** ECJ is not bound by its own previous decisions, although tends to follow them. And, only uses purposive approach to interpretation of EU law.
- Mainly deal with **disputes** concerning member states and EU institutions breaching EU law – **not individual citizens.**

ROLE: (function) *contained in A220 of Treaty of Rome*
To ensure that EU law is applied, and uniformly so, in all member states - by:

1. **hearing disputes** concerning breaches of EU law by member states / EU institutions.
2. **Giving Preliminary Rulings** as to the **validity** and **meaning** of EU law – in response to A234 referrals from member state court / tribunal.

Article 234 Referrals: [ECJ]

➢ Article 234 of the Treaty of Rome sets out the procedure for:
- o **courts and tribunals in member states**
- o **to ask the ECJ to clarify the meaning &/or validity of a piece of EU law.**

➢ The ECJ's answer is called a **"preliminary ruling"** :
- o it is **a judgment which must be followed in all member states**; not merely their opinion.

➢ *This enables the ECJ to fulfil their role: to ensure that all EU law is interpreted and applied in the same way, in all member states. Hence achieving uniformity. This is the pivotal role that the ECJ performs in the success of the EU.*

The issue is when should the member state court / tribunal make such a referral?

Must make a referral from national court from which there is no further appeal
e.g. House of Lords

In all lower courts it is up to the judge whether or not to make a referral:

A dispute is resolved by applying the facts of the case to the relevant law. If a piece of EU law is being applied the judge can interpret himself, or he can "stay" the proceedings (put case on hold) and make an A234 referral to the ECJ. Applying their interpretation to the case before him when he receives their preliminary ruling. **This causes a delay to the case and increases the costs**. For this reason English judges have been reluctant to make too many referrals. Equally, the ECJ does not wish to become overloaded with giving preliminary rulings to 25 member states!

o **ECJ have held that:** *[As stated in Costa v ENEL (1964)]*
An A234 ruling should only be made where EU law is crucial to resolving the case, and not if there has been a previous ruling on the issue from the ECJ.

In *Foglia v Novello (1980)* the ECJ held that there must be a dispute. Clarifying that an A234 referral can only be made if there is a case before the national court / tribunal – and that EC law is crucial to resolving the case.

o In an English case, Bingham J stated that the ECJ is better suited to interpreting EU law purposively and re-iterated the ECJ's view on when a referral should be made by a member state court. *[Samex case in 1983]*

o In contrast, Lord Denning, in *Bulmer v Bollinger (1974)* felt there should be a further guideline: if the court believes the EU law is reasonably clear and free from doubt, then no referral needs to be made.

o This view was recently declared by the ECJ in *Gaston Schul v Netherlands, ECJ (C461-03):* **Held that a referral must be made unless the question is irrelevant to the outcome of the case / has already been answered by the court / the answer is so obvious as to leave no scope for reasonable doubt.**

STAGE 1

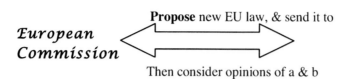

Propose new EU law, & send it to

European Commission

a. *Economic & Social Committee*
b. *European Parliament*

Then consider opinions of a & b

STAGE 2

European Commission   **Draft** legislation and send it to   *European Council*

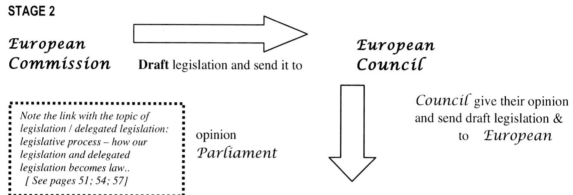

Council give their opinion and send draft legislation & to *European*

> Note the link with the topic of legislation / delegated legislation: legislative process – how our legislation and delegated legislation becomes law..
> [See pages 51; 54; 57]

opinion
Parliament

European Parliament Have **3 options:**

1. *APPROVE*   Then *Council* **passes** the draft legislation (becomes law)

2. *AMEND*   Then *Council* **review and may accept** the draft legislation

3. **REJECT**   Then *Council* **must be unanimous in order to pass** the legislation

The European Parliament's decisions are persuasive, not binding on the European Council.

> The EU's legislation-making process involves 3 main institutions:
> European Parliament – which represents the EU's citizens
> European Council – which represents the individual member states
> The European Commission – which seeks to uphold the interests of the Union as a whole. This 'institutional triangle' produces the policies and laws that apply throughout the EU. In principle, it is the Commission that proposes new laws, but it is the Parliament and Council that adopt them.

The European Council passes: (under A249 Treaty of Rome)   [laws made by EU Council:]

Regulations   **Binding in their entirety**
- o   **law in all member states the moment they are passed by Council**
- o   regulations confer rights and impose obligations upon individuals in member states

Directives   **Binding as to the result to be achieved**
- o   obligation upon member states to pass law to give effect to the content of the directive
- o   **not law until member state until passes law to give effect to directive**
- o   directives impose obligation upon member state (to which it is addressed), to create rights

Decisions   **Binding in their entirety upon those to whom they are addressed.**
They can be addressed to all member states generally they concern specific people or institutions, hence often addressed to corporations in particular member states.

Opinions   **Have no binding force, but are persuasive** [may be followed]

TERMINOLOGY:

DIRECTLY APPLICABLE:
- ➤ **Automatically become law in all member states the moment they are created**.
- ➤ Hence, ensure law is uniform across all Member states.
- ➤ **can be relied upon by individuals in courts / tribunals in member states**
  Hence, is said to have

- ➤ **DIRECT EFFECT in member states:**
- ➤ Law enforceable directly in member state courts, the moment is is made.

TYPES OF LAW:

TREATIES: Highest source of EU law
- ○ **Outline the role and powers of the EU institutions**
- ○ **State the objectives of the EU**
- ○ **Can introduce substantive law** e.g. A141 of Treaty of Rome: equal pay for men & women
  Create rights and impose obligations
  Treaties are <u>directly applicable</u> –   in all member states.

[directly applicable in our English legal system by virtue of s2(1) European Communities Act 1972]

REGULATIONS: like treaties:
Confer rights / impose obligations upon individuals in member states.
Binding in their entirety -   are **<u>directly</u> applicable**

- • ECJ held in ***Van Gend En Loos (1963***) that regulations are directly applicable if they are sufficiently clear, precise and unconditional; that they create an "enforceable community right" for the client which can be enforced through national courts.
- • in Taittinger v Allbev (1994), the Court of Appeal applied EU Regulation 823/87, regarding the labeling of wine, to grant the injunction sought by the plaintiff champagne makers, against the defendants selling "Elderflower Champagne".

DIRECTIVES: unlike regulations & treaties:
impose obligation upon member state (to which it is addressed), to create rights (for individuals in that member state)
Binding as to the result to be achieved i.e. **NOT <u>directly</u> applicable**
They are not law in member state until that member state passes law to give effect to the directive – hence individuals cannot enforce rights mentioned in Directive until member states creates the rights in law [implements the directive].

- • **Once implemented, an individual can rely upon the rights in the national (implementing) law – no need to enforce the EU directive use national law**
  - ○ <u>E.g. statutory instrument:</u> Unfair Terms in Consumer Contracts Regulations 1994 implements an EU directive giving consumers rights of protection from unfair terms in contracts. <u>e.g. Act:</u> Consumer Protection Act 1987 was passed to implement an EU directive on liability for defective products.
- • **The problem is if the member state does NOT implement (give effect to) the directive – if member state does not create the law for individuals to enforce rights mentioned in EU directive.**

Regulations & Directives are both made by EU Institutions, *by virtue of A249 Treaty of Rome*

The main problem is that the **bulk of EU law is in form of directives, which require member states to implement the directive into their national law before individuals can rely upon the rights** (to be achieved in the directive) in their national courts (as a source of law).

       Uniformity can only be achieved if all member states do implement the directive. The EU relies upon the European Commission and the ECJ to ensure that directives are implemented: *e.g. In Commission v Greece (2000), Greece was called to account for non-implementation of directives 75/442 & 78/319 – re: waste disposal – and ordered to pay a penalty of €20,000 per day until it implemented the directives into its national law.*

The_**ECJ created** the **principles** of **Direct Effect** and **Indirect Effect** in order to overcome the problems of non-implementation of directives by member states.

I.e. the ECJ created the "vehicle" to enable individuals **to rely upon the unimplemented directive, in their national courts – in certain circumstances** – in order to try to ensure uniformity of EU law throughout all member states.

The ECJ explained in Pubblico Ministero v Ratti (1979) that member states could not be allowed to rely on their own wrongful failure to implement directives as a means of denying individual rights.

VERTICAL DIRECT EFFECT:

where **individuals** can use the EU legislation [which is not directly applicable] in national courts to enforce rights **against state or "emanation of state"**

HORIZONTAL DIRECT EFFECT:

Where **individuals** can use the EU legislation [which is not directly applicable] in national courts to enforce rights **against other individuals**.

PRINCIPLE OF DIRECT EFFECT:

Enforceability of directives in national courts
Through A234 Preliminary Rulings the ECJ have held:

1 _**Directives can have direct effect -   If sufficiently clear, precise and unconditional**
      Van Duyn v Home Office (1974)

2 Only IF implementation date of directive has expired (& still unimplemented)
      Ratti case (1979)

3 Directives only have <u>vertical</u> direct effect
      i.e. unimplemented directives can **only be relied upon** in national court **by an <u>individual</u> when the case is <u>against</u> "state or emanation of state"** – if the directive has not been implemented - & the directive is clear, precise and unconditional (directive constitutes a complete legal obligation capable of enforcement by a court.)   *Marshall case (1986)*

English courts have interpreted "emanation of the state" to include:
      police force   *Johnston v Chief Constable Royal Ulster Constabulary (1986)*
      Local authority   *Re London Boroughs case (1990)*
      Tax authorities   *Becker case (1982)*
      Bodies responsible for state funded health care –
            Marshall v Southampton & South West Hampshire Area Health Authority (1986)

As directives only have vertical direct effect, the ECJ principle of Direct Effect only overcomes the problems of non-implementation of directives for individuals wishing to enforce such rights against the state (or emanation of the state).
It does not enable the same rights to be enforced against anyone other than the state (e.g. a private company / individual).

Potential for injustice: DUE TO DIRECTIVES ONLY HAVING VERTICAL DIRECT EFFECT

Injustice: employee in public sector may be able to rely upon direct effect to obtain rights in directives to challenge employer in national court – but not an employee in private sector. As illustrated in the following cases:

> *Foster v British Gas (1991) HL,* applied ECJ preliminary ruling that **"emanation of state" includes a body which the state has made responsible for providing a public service, and which has special powers to do so.** HL held this definition covered British Gas, therefore Mrs Foster could rely upon the unimplmented Equal Treatment Directive (using direct effect) to receive compensation for being made redundant before men would be.

> However, in *Doughty v Rolls Royce (1992) CA,* Rolls Royce was not held to be within the definition of "emanation of state", although in public ownership Rolls Royce was not providing a public service – hence Doughty could not rely upon the unimplemented directive in UK court. Also, in *Duke v GEC Reliance (1988),* Mrs Duke was not able to rely upon the unimplemented Equal Treatment Directive as her employer was a private company – and directives do not have horizontal direct effect.

Therefore, to overcome this problem:

ECJ developed principle of Indirect Effect:

> *Van Colson case (1984)* – **national implementing legislation must be interpreted "in the light of the wording and purpose of the directive" – to give effect to EU law**

> *Marleasing case (1990) –* **all national legislation must be interpreted, "wherever possible", in the "light of EU law".**
> [to achieve member states duty of community law loyalty – contained in Article 5 of the Treaty of Rome]

Only problem is if there is no national legislation to interpret "in light" of the directive.

Possible action: sue the member state for failing to implement the directive.

– in *Francovich v Italian State (1991)* ECJ held that an individual who suffers loss due to the state's failure to implement a directive may have an **action for damages against the state** (for the loss suffered).

See summary on next page

Example of problems of non-implementation of directives:

EU issues a directive – imposing obligation upon member state to implement certain rights for individuals in that member state, within a stated time.

e.g. <u>Working Time Directive</u> **issued in 1993, which imposed obligation upon UK to enable individuals to enforce rights regarding number of hours / rest periods / holidays ... re: work. With an implementation date of 1995. The UK did not implement this directive until 1998.**

1993 – 1995 individual cannot use the directive to enforce such rights.

1995 – 1998 **Once the time limit for the implementation of a Directive has expired** individual can enforce the rights, using principle of ***vertical direct effect***.
- **only against "state or emanation of the state"** *[Marshall case (1986)]*
- i.e. public company providing a public service

[but not against private company – directives do not have horizontal direct effect]
- **and only if the rights are clear, precise and unconditional.**
- As seen in *Gibson v West Riding of Yorkshire Council (1999)* where swimming instructor used direct effect to rely upon the unimplemented Working Time Directive and successfully claim compensation for non-payment of paid holidays.

<u>Against private company / individual:</u>
Principle of ***indirect effect*** may enable use of directive in national court against private company or other individual. *[Marleasing case (1990]*
- **Only if there is national legislation which can be interpreted to give effect to the unimplemented directive** – interpreted "in light of the wording and purpose of the directive"

OR

Using Francovitch (1991) ruling, **the individual may sue the government for non-implementation of the directive,** in action to recover damages for loss suffered – if rights are clear, precise and unconditional & is causal link between non-implementation of rights and loss suffered.

From 1998 Use the national legislation [Act or Statutory Instrument] which has been created in order to implement the rights contained within the Working Time Directive.

Note: Marshall v Southampton & South West Hampshire Area Health Authority (1986)
- Illustrates English courts use of Article 234 Referral (to ECJ)
- Illustrates ECJ's ruling that directives only have vertical direct effect
- Illustrates supremacy of EU law

Miss Marshall, aged 62, was dismissed from her post as a dietician under the Area Health Authority's policy for retirement: men at 65, women at 60; which mirrored the age at which state retirement pensions became payable. This policy was contrary to the Equal Treatment Directive 76/207, yet was not discriminatory under Sex Discrimination Act 1975: i.e. conflicting national and EU law. Miss Marshall successfully sued for compensation for unfair dismissal, relying upon the unimplemented directive using the principle of vertical direct effect. The UK legislation was later amended to conform with the directive.

Supremacy of EC law:

➤ First established by ECJ in Van Gen en Loos case (1963)
➤ Supreme, even over national law made after that EC law – Costa v ENEL (1964)
➤ Article 5 Treaty of Rome states DUTY OF LOYALTY to EU by member states (and EU Institutions)
➤ [remember that the prerequisite of the effectiveness of EU law is that it must become part of the national law – hence principles of direct & indirect effect, and ruling in Francovich – see page 36]]
➤ ECJ preliminary ruling in Johnson case (1986): duty of national courts to seek to interpret national law to conform with EU law, and if this was not possible, to enforce EU law itself in preference to national law, through the doctrine of direct effect. Restated by ECJ in its preliminary ruling to House of Lords in Factortame case (1990); emphasising supremacy of EU law over national law.

UK's viewpoint:
  o **McCarthys** Ltd v Smith (1981)
        Lord Denning – **"it is our bounden duty to give priority to EC law"**
  o **Garland** v British Rail Engineering Ltd (1983)
        Lord Diplock endorsed Lord Denning's view - Held statute passed after EC law should be interpreted in light of EC law
  o **Pickstone** v Freemans plc (1989)
        House of Lords emphasised **the need to interpret English law, where possible, so as to comply with EU law.**

In none of the above cases did the House of Lords actually confront the constitutional issue of direct conflict between EC law and UK law! – preferred to focus upon the interpretation of national law rather than the matter of disapplying national law in favour of EU law.

Limitations on English Parliamentary Sovereignty:

By joining the EU we have limited our sovereignty:
  o Parliament should **uphold the duty of EU loyalty**, in Article 5 of the Treaty of Rome; and not pass legislation which conflicts with EU law – **hence limiting the ability of Parliament to make any law it likes.** (sovereignty – see page 1).
  o As stated by the ECJ in Van Gend en loos (1963) *"creation of a new legal order ... for the benefit of which the states have limited their sovereign rights"*

EUROPEAN COMMUNITIES ACT 1972:

S2   **Enshrines concept of direct effect** – applicability of EC law in English law
        And
        Provides that **English law should be interpreted and have effect subject to the principle of supremacy of EC law.**

S3   **UK accepted Binding authority of ECJ rulings and principles**

Note:
  o some constitutional lawyers argue that the binding effect of EU law comes from the ECA 1972; an Act of Parliament which can be repealed – although at the moment Parliament chooses not to.
  o The courts have declined comment upon the conflict between EU supremacy and national Parliamentary Sovereignty; choosing instead to resolve the problems of conflicting laws through purposive interpretation of national legislation in line with EU law.

Exam Question on EUROPEAN LAW:

1   (a)   Describe and illustrate with cases the Article 234 reference procedure.

       (b)   In each of the following situations, consider whether an English court would have either a **duty** or a **power** to refer a question to the European Court of Justice:

            (i)   Jack has made a claim in an Employment Tribunal to an issue of law covered by the Working Time Directive. Clarification of a key point contained in the Directive is likely to resolve the case.

            (ii)   A mobile phone company has appealed its case on 'unfair terms' in consumer contracts as far as the House of Lords. The Court of Appeal has already accepted that an interpretation of European Law would decide the outcome of the case.

            (iii)   A case relating to restrictions on Sunday trading is put before a magistrates' court. An article 234 reference in *Torfaen Borough Council v B & Q (1990)* has already identified that such restrictions were in breach of the Treaty of Rome.

       (c)   Explain the role of the ECJ and discuss the ways in which it has been 'fundamental in ensuring the enforcement of Treaties through many landmark cases, and in ensuring uniform applications of European Community Law.
OCR AS Level Law, January 2004, Q1

New specification specimen question: [see page 11 for example of a question]
Question with 3 parts: a, b, c,   *which must be answered <u>with reference to the source</u> (printed material) provided – total of 60 marks.*

      a)   12 marks … AO1 … "describe, explain"
      b)   15 marks … AO2 … 3 problem scenarios to apply law to.
      c)   27 marks in total, split as follows:
         c   (i)   15 marks – AO1 - "describe"; &
         c   (ii)   12 marks – AO2 - " discuss, comment upon …"
[6 marks for AO3 which is global for the paper]
[a total of 60 raw marks [40% of total AS Law marks]

European Law may be examined on its own, or along with law reform or statutory interpretation or judicial precedent or legislation / delegated legislation.
See page 11 for example of new specification question on delegated legislation and European Law.

Previous exam questions on European law have been along the following lines:
Asking you to explain vertical and horizontal direct effect
Asking you to describe the law making functions of the European Commission / European Parliament / European Council
Asking you to discuss the problems of non-implementation of directives
Asking you to compare the differences between Treaties, Regulations, Directives and Decisions
Asking you to explain A234 referrals to the ECJ

Outline of new AS Unit 1 examination paper:
English Legal System [G141]
For OCR exam board

The exam paper will include 2 sections:

Section A

Containing **5 essay-based questions**
Each containing 2 parts:
- o a) describe ... for 18 marks [AO1 knowledge], and
- o b) discuss ... for 9 marks [AO2 evaluation]
- o 3 marks across the question for AO3 (grammar, logical sequence, structure of answers)

Section B

Containing **2 application-style questions**
Each containing 2 parts:
- o a) describe ... for 18 marks [AO1 knowledge], and
- o b) explain / apply ... for 9 marks [AO2 evaluation / application]
- o 3 marks across the question for AO3 (grammar, logical sequence, structure of answers)

Students must answer a total of 4 questions
Choosing at least 1 question from Section A and 1 question from Section B
- ➢ The exam is for two hours
- ➢ A total of 120 marks for this paper
- ➢ Forming 60% of the AS law examination

Section A and B questions are based upon the following OCR AS Law specification headings / topics:

1 **Civil courts and ADR** (alternative dispute resolution)

2 **Police Powers**

3 **Pre-trial matters and appeals**

4 **Sentencing**

5 **The Judiciary**

6 **The Legal Professions** (solicitors and barristers)

7 **Lay People** (magistrates and juries)

8 **Government funding and legal advice.**

Examples of the new specification exam questions can be seen on pages 50, 63, 73, 78, 99.

Note: *An outline of the OCR Unit 2 paper: Sources of Law, can be found at the front of this book,*
following the "contents" page

Police Powers

The police need the legal right to stop, search, arrest, detain and interview individuals against their will, in order to investigate crime – gather evidence.

PACE 1984   Police and Criminal Evidence Act 1984, as amended, contains the **police powers** (legal right e.g. to stop individuals). It also contains **rights** for those individuals, as a **safeguard** against abuse of police power.

PACE defines the legal exercise of police powers, if PACE is not followed the power was unlawfully used, with the following consequences for the individual:

- possible inadmissibility of any evidence at trial
  - [material evidence S78 and confession S76]
- individual can complain to police complaints authority
- individual may sue the police (civil) for false imprisonment

Codes of Practice, drawn up by the Home Secretary under S66 PACE, provide extra detail on the provisions PACE. These Codes do not form part of the law, however breach of these Codes can give rise to disciplinary action. PACE 1984 was amended recently by Serious Organised Crime and Police Act 2005 [SOCAP]

Away from the station

Power to **stop and search**, and to **arrest** an individual,
<u>in the following circumstances</u>:

> Serious Organised Crime and Police Act 2005, ss116-118, enables police, away from the station, to take photographs of a person; fingerprints and footwear impressions.

S1 PACE 1984   Stop and Search

> **Police power:**   S1:   *to stop and search:*
>
> - A **person / vehicle**;
>
> - In a **public place**;
>
> - In order to search for **stolen or prohibited articles**
>   - *(includes offensive weapons and "tools of the trade")*
>   - *(includes prohibited fireworks – since SOCAP, 2005)*
>
> - <u>**If have REASONABLE GROUNDS to believe they will find such articles**</u>   *(not randomly stop & search)*

Safeguards:

- S2 police officer must **give name / station and reason** for search

- S2(a) **Only ask remove outer clothing** – coat, hat, gloves …

- S3 police officer must make **written record** of search asap

> Osman V DPP (1999)
> Held: stop & search by police officers unlawful – as the officer did not give name, station and reason for search - hence Mr Osman was found not guilty of assaulting the police in execution of their duty.

"reasonable grounds"

This is the **main safeguard** against abuse of police powers, defined as follows:

- **S1(3) PACE, must be more than mere suspicion**
  House of Lords in Hussein case in 1970, Lord Devlin: mere suspicion or hunch is insufficient

- **Code A – objective test ...** would reasonable person expect to find ...
  As affirmed by CA in Castorina v Chief Constable of Surrey (1988)
- Code A – **should not be based on personal factors alone ...**
  e.g. not on race / age / dress / known criminal record ... alone

- Reasonable grounds must be apparent before stop and search
- *O'Hara v Chief Constable of the Royal Ulster Constabulary (1996):*
  House of Lords held 2-stage test: actual suspicion (subjective test) and reasonable grounds for that suspicion (objective test).

NOTE: Always remember to relate reasonable grounds to the police power you are describing – e.g to state what is the police officer must have reasonable grounds to believe in relation to the section of PACE (police power) you are describing:
E.g.   S1   reasonable grounds to believe will find stolen or prohibited articles
E.g   S24   reasonable grounds to believe: have /in act of/about to : commit an offence

---

NOTE: **Evaluation of S1**

➢ Despite Code A guidance, still evidence police do stop & search on personal factors alone:
➢ black people 6 times more likely be stopped and searched than other groups of people – Home Office Statistics, 2003. E.g. black Lord Taylor complained of frequently being stopped whilst out jogging.
➢ Arguably one's civic duty to bear the inconvenience – another to be stopped regularly.
➢ In 1996 only 12% of those stop and searched were then arrested.
➢ However, is also evidence that increases in stop & searches can lead to reduction in crime

Other powers to stop and search:

- Misuse of Drugs Act 1971 – to search for controlled drugs /   Prevention Terrorism Act

- S60 CJPOA 1994 – in anticipation of violence - no need reasonable grounds to believe ....

- Road Checks – If Superintendent authorises, if reasonable suspicion suspect committed serious arrestable offence is at large – under S4 PACE S4

The police can lawfully arrest an individual either by obtaining a warrant from the magistrates,
OR   under PACE 1984, without a warrant – (arrest straight away):

SOCAP 2005 amended PACE, so that today:
all offences to be arrestable, without warrant   [by police under S24 PACE]
BUT subject to a <u>necessity</u> test

S24 PACE   for **any offence**
police have power to arrest, **without warrant**, any person:

- Who is **about to** commit / is **in act of** committing / **has committed** <u>any</u> <u>offence</u>
<u>OR</u>
- There are **reasonable grounds** for suspecting one of these occurrences
                              [even if no offence is actually committed]
<u>AND</u>
  - ONLY IF they believe it is **<u>necessary to arrest</u>** - without a warrant
To be lawful arrest, one of the following reasons must apply – making arrest necessary:

TO PREVENT:
> Physical injury, loss or damage to property, causing an offence against public decency, obstruction of the highway, any prosecution being hindered by the disappearance of the person in question.

TO ENABLE:
> The name and address of suspect to be ascertained

TO PROTECT:
> A vulnerable person
> To protect a child (or vulnerable person)

> **Necessary to arrest, there and then, on the street, without a warrant.**

[guidance in new Code G: Code of Practice, Jan 06]
NOTE: Reasonable grounds / belief has same definition as for Stop and search (above):
Actual suspicion on part of Police officer and reasonable grounds for that suspicion – as in guidance notes in Code G

Safeguards: The police officer must:
(otherwise arrest is unlawful)

> ***Christie v Lechinsky (1947)***
>
> HL Held precise technical language not needed provided substance of offence brought to attention of person arrested
>
> e.g. "You're nicked for mugging" is sufficient.

- **S28** **Tell** suspect he/she is under arrest
& **give reason** for arrest

- **S30** Take to P Station as soon as practicable
after arrest

- Identify themselves if not in uniform (to make arrest lawful)

- **Caution** the individual they are arresting.

- Note, S117   **Reasonable force** may be used.

ARREST

Arrest at common law:
- **Police** have power to enter premises and arrest for **Breach of the Peace**
- *Bibby v Chief Constable of Essex Police (2000)*
- Court of Appeal summarised when this power can be used:
  - o Sufficient real threat to peace
  - o From person to be arrested
  - o Whose conduct clearly interferes with rights of others
  - o Unreasonable conduct.

> *Nicol v DPP (1996)* Blowing of horns, throwing twigs into the water by animal rights activists, to persuade anglers to stop fishing during an angling contest was Held to be breach of the peace – unreasonable behaviour.

Other powers of arrest, for police:
- S46A PACE, [as amended by CJPOA 1994]   arrest for **breaching bail conditions**
- CJPOA 1994, power to arrest for collective & aggravated trespass in connection with offences committed in **preparing for or attending a "rave",** or intentional harassment.

S24A PACE   gives **private citizen** power to arrest, without warrant:

- anyone they believe is about to commit / is in act of committing / has committed **an "indictable" offence.**

- IF they believe it is **necessary** to arrest (there and then) – i.e. in order to prevent:
  - ➢ Physical injury to the person or others
  - ➢ Loss of / damage to property
  - ➢ That person disappearing

Note:

1   (confusingly) "indictable" is defined as all offences which may be tried on indictment in the Crown court – i.e. indictable and triable-either-way offences.

2   Private citizens beware!
If an "indictable" offence has not been committed the   arrest itself will be unlawful – and you may be liable for damages!.
> R v Self (1992), arrest by store detective held unlawful as defendant found innocent of offence of theft – hence could not be guilty of assault with intent to resist arrest.

Power to **detain, interview** and **search** an individual, **in the following circumstances**:
Volunteer free leave at any time – S29
- If arrested, under S37 can detain in order to gather evidence: material /confession
- Individual being detained is the responsibility of custody sergeant

Powers

> **Custody officer monitors detention** & keeps custody record to ensure PACE and Codes of Practice adhered to.
>
> **Detention clock** starts when arrive at police station.
>
> **Detention is reviewed** by Inspector at 9 hourly intervals to ensure grounds for detention still exist i.e. not merely

DETENTION: *in order to gather evidence: search / confession*

- **How long an individual can be detained, against their will.**
- **If they have been lawfully arrested.**
- At the end of each detention period, the police must either release or charge *Note: if charge the issue of bail arises.*
PACE 1984, as amended by SOCAP 2005:-

For any offence*:*
- **S41**   detain for **36 hours**

For any "indictable" offence*:* *[triable-either-way or indictable]*
- **S42**   detain for **further 12 hours if permission of superintendent**
- **S43**   detain for **total of 96 hours if permission of magistrates.**

Note: detention under suspicion of terrorism does not fall under PACE.

Whilst being lawfully detained at the police station, PACE 1984 gives the police the power, in certain circumstances, to carry out / and take:

both INTIMATE and NON-INTIMATE
SEARCHES and SAMPLES

SEARCH:
- **S54** gives the police the **power to search** an arrested person, at the police station, and **seize items** which they reasonably believe **might be used to injure anyone**, or used to make an escape, or are evidence.

- **S55** gives the police the power to carry out **intimate searches** if authorised by a superintendent – if he reasonably believes a weapon or drug is concealed. This search must carried out **by a registered doctor or nurse**.

SAMPLES:
- **S61** gives the police the power to take **fingerprints**.
- **S62** gives the police the power to take **non-intimate samples**, e.g. hair / nail clippings / & saliva

Both of the above samples do not require the individual's consent.

- **S63** gives the police the power to take **intimate samples**, e.g. blood / saliva / semen. These samples must be taken by a registered doctor.

INTERVIEW:

Questioning the individual, in the hope of obtaining a confession – seen as reliable evidence by magistrates and jury alike**.**

RIGHTS: protection for individual - what the police must do to protect individuals rights

Tape record interview	Under **S60** PACE, unless purely summary offence, to ensure confession is not coerced
Telephone call	Under Code C detained individual should be allowed to make a telephone call
Right to have **someone informed** of their detention at police station	Under **S56** PACE, person individual chooses must be told of the arrest, and where they are being held, without delay when individual arrives at police station
Right **to consult with** a legal adviser (**solicitor**)	Under **S58**, an individual held in custody is entitled to consult privately with a solicitor, and free of charge (duty solicitor)
An **"appropriate adult"**	PACE and Code C state **that those under 17 years of age or mentally disordered / handicapped** must have a parent or social worker with them whilst being interviewed by police.

- THE RIGHT TO A SOLICITOR & TO HAVE SOMEONE INFORMED:

> [S56 & S58] **can be delayed**
> **for up to 36 hours**

IF: *Senior officer* has *reasonable grounds* to believe this right might lead to interference with evidence / persons, or alert others involved in offence, or hinder recovery of property.

However: The Court of Appeal, in R v Sammuel [1988] Held that **such delay can only be justified on rare occasions** – that S58 / consulting with a solicitor, is a "fundamental freedom".

Note that in R v Grant in 2005, a conviction was quashed following evidence that the police had eavesdropped on conversations with solicitor – "affront to integrity"

NOTE: Code C   [code of practice]
                 contains **guidelines as to treatment of suspect** whilst in detention:
                 o   With regard to: meals / exercise / sleep –
                 o   & the right to read copy of Codes of Practice!

Further safeguards: At the police station

1. **REVIEW** of detention and Custody record.

2. **LIMITS TO length of detention** and Limitations **on search and samples.**

3. **CODE C**   contains **guidelines as to TREATMENT of suspect** whilst in detention:
    o   With regard to: meals / exercise / sleep - & right to read copy of Codes of Practice!

4. **CAUTION:**
    <u>inform suspect of loss of right to silence & possible consequences:</u> before questioned.
    The detained individual **cannot be forced to speak,**
    but there are **four situations** where if the individual does not answer questions
    the **court can draw "adverse inference" [guilt] from silence:**

    o   **since Criminal Justice and Public Order Act 1994:**
    o   **facts** which they later rely on in their defence [S34];
    o   fail to account for **objects/marks** on their clothing [S36];
    o   fail to account for their **presence at a particular place** [S37];
    o   OR if remain **silent during trial.** [S35]
    o

5. **EXCLUSION OF EVIDENCE:**
    At court: court may declare evidence obtained by breach of PACE inadmissible at trial:
    e.g. any evidence obtained through unlawful stop& search / arrest / detention …

    confession S76

    o   **cannot be admitted** at trial **if obtained by "oppression"** of person who made it,
        or in consequence of anything said or done which was likely in the
        circumstances, to render it unreliable
    o   S67(8) PACE defined "oppression" as torture, inhuman or degrading treatment
    o   R v Fulling (1987) "oppression" to be given its dictionary meaning: i.e. exercise of
        power or authority in burdensome, harsh or wrongful manner
    o   R v Miller (1992) being asked same question over 300 times Held to be oppressive
    .

    material evidence S78

    o   **Discretion of judge** - whether to allow submission of material evidence
        improperly obtained.
    o   **If court believe to include evidence would have adverse effect on fairness of
        proceedings.**

Exam Questions on police powers

1 Describe the powers of the police to stop and search and arrest an individual on the street.
    OCR AS Level Law, January 2005, Q1

2 Fred has been arrested and taken to the police station on suspicion of murdering Wilma.
   Discuss whether Fred's rights are adequately protected whilst at the police station during detention, searches and interviews.
    OCR AS Level Law, January 2005, Q5

New specification specimen question: [see examples on pages 63, 73, 78, 99]

3 (a) Describe the powers the police have to stop and search an individual in the street   [18]

   (b) Tyrone, aged 16, has missed the last bus and has to walk home. It is 2am and a police officer driving past in a police car sees Tyrone and stops. The police officer tells Tyrone to empty his pockets and Tyrone refuses. The police officer then grabs Tyrone's shoulder, pushes him into the police car and takes him to the local police station.

        Advise Tyrone on whether the police officer acted lawfully with regard to stop and search and the arrest.   [9]

        OCR AS Level Law, Q6 specimen paper G141QP.
        total 30 marks;

                                                    AO1 18 marks in (a)
                                                    AO2 9 marks in (b)
                                                    AO3 3 marks across both (a)

Pre-trail hearings – take place in the magistrates' court

- For all offences: **EAH** – early administration hearing
  Magistrates decide whether issues of Bail / Reports / Legal Funding need to be resolved before a trial can commence.

- **for triable-either-way offences -   Mode of Trial hearing**

The category of offence dictates the court for trial.:
SUMMARY OFFENCES   - TRIED IN MAGISTRATES' COURT.
INDICTABLE OFFENCES – TRIED IN CROWN COURT
Triable-either-way offences may be tried in either court! –
tried summarily before Magistrates' court, or on indictment in Crown court.
This is because they may be committed in a minor or serious way.
E.g. theft of a mars bar / theft of a million pounds.
Therefore, there are a number of possible pre-trial hearings in order to decide which court for trial,
just for triable-either-way offences:-
         Plea before venue   & Mode of trial

> **Different personnel in each court:**
> <u>Magistrates court</u>: it is the magistrates who decide issues of conviction (guilt / innocence) and that of sentencing (punishment).
> <u>Crown court</u>: it is the jury who decide the issue of conviction and the judge who decides upon the sentence.

<u>**MODE OF TRIAL:**</u>   This the pre-trial hearing where the magistrates decide if they are willing to hear the case or not – to accept jurisdiction, or not. **If Magistrates decline jurisdiction then the defendant has no choice – the trial will be held in Crown court.**

How Mags decide:

- <u>**S19 Magistrates Court Act 1980:**</u> magistrates should **consider:**
  - **Nature and seriousness of offence**
  - Their **sentencing powers** - maximum of 12 months custodial; £5,000 fine
  - Whether defendant has legal representation
  - Since CJA 2003 Magistrates are told defendant's **prior convictions**.

- And; **Lord Chief Justice - <u>Mode of Trial Guidelines 1995</u>:**
  - **Should decline jurisdiction – send to Crown for trial IF:**
  - Complex question of law / fact involved
  - Breach of trust by defendant
  - Crime by organised gang
  - Amount involved is greater than twice the amount the magistrates can order as a fine.

- And; <u>**S19(4) MCA 1980:**</u>
  - If Attorney General or DPP are prosecuting and they want case in Crown court the magistrates must decline jurisdiction

Note:
The more serious offences, requiring harsher sentences, should be declined by Magistrates – i.e. sent Crown court

---

Defendant can choose which court for trial if<u>:</u>

If :   D Pleads not guilty *at <u>plea before venue hearing</u>*   *[If plead guilty the defendant will go for trial (sentencing) at Magistrates court - no need for the jury at Crown court to consider conviction issue.]*
And: magistrates accept jurisdiction *at <u>mode of trial hearing</u>*
If the magistrates accept jurisdiction:Since CJA 2003, the magistrates must give **indication of sentence** likely to give AND Defendant must be **warned** that Magistrates **can send case to Crown court for sentencing**

Defendant's choice revolves around two issues:

Conviction   who is most likely to believe defendant and acquit him/her?
Sentencing   if found guilty, who is most likely to order more lenient sentence?

- HIGHER ACQUITTAL RATE BY JURY, IN CROWN COURT
    - **Jury** members usually only sit once, if at all, and are more representative of society than magistrates – hence jury members tend to **be more likely to relate to / believe defendant and hence acquit:**
    - A study by Vennard: 57% acquitted in Crown / 30% in Magistrates.
    - **Magistrates** said to be **"case hardened"** often hearing similar cases less likely to believe defendant, also said to be **prosecution biased.**

- MAGISTRATES' SENTENCING POWERS LIMITED
    - Magistrates sentencing powers limited by virtue of the court: currently **maximum custodial sentence of 12 months and fine of max £5,000.**
    - **However, magistrates can send case to Crown for sentencing!**
    - Judge (in Crown court) can give maximum provided in statute for the offence (e.g. Theft 7 years custodial), and RCCJ noted judges three times more likely to give a custodial sentence than magistrates.
    - However, Magistrates criticised for their inconsistency in sentencing – similar cases often given vastly different sentences.

- DELAY - IF OPT FOR CROWN COURT TRIAL
    - **Benefits those remanded in custody who believe they will be found guilty:** more privileges and likely in prison close to home as remand prisoner, plus time on remand taken off custodial sentence
    - **Seen as manipulation of the system** when many defendants then change their plea to guilty when they reach the Crown court!

> Both Magistrates and Juries are said to be "Trial by one's peers" – which is one's fundamental right.
> However, more likely to find "one's peer" in jury; but neither are totally representative of society!

COMMITTAL PROCEEDINGS:
- **For all serious triable-either-way offences to be tried at Crown Court**
- This is a **further pre-trial hearing**, in Magistrates' Court
- Where **Magistrates decide if there is sufficient evidence for trial** - for the prosecution to prove guilt beyond a reasonable doubt.
- However, **today this is a mere formality** as the CPS [Crown Prosecution Service] carry out this task when deciding whether or not to prosecute the defendant.

PLEA and DIRECTIONS HEARING
- **This is pre-trial hearing, at Crown Court** [since Crime & Disorder Act 1988]
- **For all cases to be tried at Crown Court**
- **To ensure "all is ready for trial"**
    - **Plea** – where defendant pleads [guilty or not guilty]
    - **Directions** – issues of:
    - Number of witnesses
    - Facts admitted by both sides
    - Issues of law likely to arise – judge can rule upon before trial begins; e.g. admissibility of evidence issues
    - Then judge sets date for trial
    - Sometimes there is a further pre-trial hearing – a more detailed investigation of matters to settle in order for trial to "run smoothly", without delays, once trial starts.

Whether defendant:

> **At liberty, on condition turn up at next stage of trial - granted bail,**
> **Or   Remanded in custody** (awaiting trial) [bail denied]

Bail is considered at every stage in the criminal justice process,
hence is considered by Police, Magistrates and judge in Crown court.

Balance:
defendant's civil rights (of liberty) Vs protection of the public against offenders.
> Noting that defendant should be presumed innocent.

> In 1992 a third of prison population were on remand – bail denied – often for 6 months to a year before trial; of which 60% were either acquitted or given non-custodial sentence at trial.

Bail Act 1976:

S4 General presumption : everyone has the right to bail (presumption of innocence)

If summary offence - even stronger presumption

hence only deny bail if previously failed surrender <u>and</u> reasonable grounds to believe will do so again.

Although the general presumption is that defendant will get bail,
> **CAN DENY RIGHT TO BAIL:** Ensure that you can explain:

The **Criteria** for denying bail; and **Considerations in** deciding if criteria met. [reasonable grounds]

Criteria ▬ Reasons for denying bail: ▬

Reasonable grounds to believe if granted bail, the defendant will:
- Fail to surrender to bail; or
- Commit an offence whilst on bail; or
- Interfere with witnesses, or otherwise obstruct course of justice; or
- Defendant should be kept in custody for his/her own protection

> 12% of those given bail failed to turn up at court. (Criminal Justice Statistics 2000)
>
> Nearly 25% commit at least one offence whilst on bail. (Home Office Report No.72 1998)

Considerations - Factors the court consider when assessing whether above criteria
> **apply to the defendant** – e.g. whether likely to fail to surrender
- The OFFENCE: the nature (type) and seriousness of the offence
- The DEFENDANT: his character, associations, community ties
- Strength of evidence
- Record: bail before
- Record: criminal record (previous convictions)
- Since Criminal Justice & Courts Services Act 2000: must take into account any drug use by the defendant

If Bail is granted - can impose conditions

[i.e. believe criteria may be met but not wish deny liberty/bail]
- Report to police station set day/time
- curfew
- residence at named address
- surrender passport
- surety (someone promises to pay set sum of money to court if defendant fail to turn up at next stage.)

> Note: increasing use of Bail Hostels and electronic tagging. Enabling monitoring of conditions attached to Bail.

If bail granted and then defendant fails to turn up = offence of absconding

Magistrates: up to 3 months custodial and/or fine /   Crown: up to 12 months custodial and/or fine

both defendant and prosecution can appeal bail decision.

- Defendant appeals to QBD of High court – judge in chambers
- And, since CJA 2003, Prosecution can appeal all offences punishable with imprisonment – as long as originally objected to bail and gave verbal notification of intention to appeal.

---

certain situations alter the S4 presumption
[alter the presumption of a right to bail]
seems now treat defendant as guilty until offender proved innocent!:

S26 CJPOA 1994   OFFENCE COMMITTED WHILST ON BAIL
- **no presumption of bail**   (defendant to show why bail should be granted)
- *If defendant prosecuted for Triable-either-way offence or Indictable offence,*
- *whilst on bail for another offence*

S25 CJPOA 1994   REPEAT CERTAIN SERIOUS OFFENCES
- **only grant bail in "exceptional circumstances"**
- *If defendant already been convicted of and served sentence for certain indictable offences AND now being prosecuted for any one of those offences.*   [not necessarily same offence]
- Offences of: *Murder / Rape and attempts; and manslaughter*
- This section arguably still breaches Art 5 ECHR, because it proceeds from a presumption of guilt.

CJA 2003 IMPRISONABLE OFFENCE INVOLVING DRUGS
- **only grant bail in "exceptional circumstances"**
- **if imprisonable offence and drugs involved**
- either 1   charged with possession or intent to supply
- or   2   believe misuse of Class A drug
- or   3   refused treatment

IN THE ABOVE SITUATIONS IT IS FOR DEFENDANT TO SHOW WHY BAIL SHOULD BE GRANTED – WHY WILL NOT FULFIL CRITERIA FOR DENYING BAIL

> *New specification specimen question:*
> [see examples on pages 44; 56; 65; 70]
> *The question, if on the paper, will be in the new format::*
> a. *Describe … for 18 marks AO1*
> b. *Discuss / Comment upon for 9 marks AO2*
> [total 30 marks; AO3 worth 3]

Exam Questions on pre-trial matters (hearings)

Mode of Trial:

1   Sunita has been charged with theft.
- (i)   Identify the two courts in which Sunita could be tried and who would Try her in those courts.
- (ii)   Comment on the advantages and disadvantages, to Sunita, of Choosing either court.   *OCR AS Level Law, June 2004, Q5 [20]*

Bail:

1   Bill is charged with manslaughter.
Discuss whether the criteria used by the police or the courts in deciding whether to grant him bail in such a case are satisfactory.   *OCR AS Level Law, January 2006, Q6*

2   Describe the current system of bail.   OCR AS level Law, June 2005, Q4

Mode of Trial and Bail:

1   Steve has been charged with the murder of his mother, who was dying of cancer.
Phil has been charged with the theft of £5000 worth of parts from a car accessories dealer.
- (i)   Explain how it will be decided whether bail is likely to be granted to Steve and Phil.
- (ii)   Explain how it will be decided in which court Phil will be tried and Comment on whether he should have the right to choose trial by jury.

Sentencing

The **Actual punishment** for guilty defendants.
Decided by magistrates in Magistrates' court, and Judges in Crown court.
As stated in CJA 2003 and PCCSA 2000

THIS TOPIC IS SPLIT INTO 4 MAIN AREAS:
- **TYPES** of sentence   **Actual punishments**
- **AIMS** of sentencing   Theories of **why punish**
- **LINK**   Which sentences achieve which aims
- **DISCRETION**   **How the Judge / Magistrate decides** which sentence to impose

---

TYPES OF SENTENCE - ACTUAL PUNISHMENT, as currently stated in CJA 2003.

The guilty defendant may receive one, or a mix of the following 4 main options:

DISCHARGE   *either conditionally or unconditionally – no punishment*
FINE   *payment of money – [goes to the Treasury]*
COMMUNITY SENTENCE
    With range of requirements that can be ordered - that defendant must agree to undertake
CUSTODIAL SENTENCE
    loss of liberty – prison / YO Institute / Secure Training Centre

> **Current proposal: for re-introduction of unit fine scheme.** Unit fines related to income: propose £75 max. income unit for high earners – e.g. possible 10 units for conviction of being drunk and disorderly could mean max. fine of £750 for high earners. Currently the max. fine for this offence is £200. "A fine is meant to have equal impact on the rich and poor" – Home Office – Management of Offenders and Sentencing Bill.

FINE   MONETARY PUNISHMENT

- Monetary punishment – **for least serious offences,**
- **amount depends upon court tried in / finances / adult or YO**
- A fine may be imposed for almost any offence other than murder.

The **amount** must:
- reflect **seriousness of offence**, and
- take account of **offender's means**
- and [for young offender: must also take account of **age**]

ADULT

Magistrates' court
- Limited by virtue of court to **Max £5,000**
- (some business offences are exception)
- This is the most common sentence in Magistrates court

Crown court
- **Limited only by virtue of statute for offence**
- only small number offenders receive fine in crown court

YOUNG OFFENDER

Magistrates' and Crown court:

Age limits:	Max £:
10-13 years old	£250, max
14-17 years old	£1,000 max
18-20 years old	£5,000 max

- If under 16 years, parent ordered to pay fine and parent's financial situation taken into account in deciding amount of fine ordered.

CJA 2003 – now enables Magistrates to arrange <u>automatic deduction of fine</u> from offender's earnings when imposing fine or upon failure to pay – and court able to <u>impose unpaid work or curfew requirements</u> on fine defaulter or disqualify offender from driving rather than send defaulter to prison.

CJA 2003 established a <u>single</u> community sentence – with a <u>range</u> of possible requirements – which **offender must agree to** (as they require the offender's co-operation).

These are requirements for the offender **to do or not do something**

Requirements - For offenders 16 years plus -

For some young offenders and all adults. One or more of the following requirements:

To do:
Supervision / unpaid work / an activity / attend a programme / undergo treatment / Reside at a set address.

---

1 SUPERVISION
supervision by probation officer.
6 months to 3 years
attend regular meetings. Live at home or hostel. Can specify activities for up to 60 days, &/or attend probation centre. 1997 Home Office research found 90% participants thought useful because gave them someone independent to talk to about their problems / get practical help; advice.

2 UNPAID WORK
work between 40 and 300 hours on community project,
[5-21hrs/week] unpaid work for benefit of community e.g tasks on conservation projects, canal clearance: useful work which may give offender sense of achievement and benefit community

3 ACTIVITY
Max of 60 days
Either to see a specified person at specified place, or take part in specified activities. E.g. receiving help with employment; group work on social problems; providing reparation to the victim.

4 PROGRAMME
Attend accredited course to address offending behaviour: e.g. anger management, sex offending, drug abuse

5 MENTAL HEALTH TREATMENT
Offender to undergo treatment for certain periods as part of community sentence or custodial sentence. Treatment by registered practitioner or chartered psychologist. Only order if satisfied such treatment is needed and may held. Requires offender's consent.

6 ALCOHOL TREATMENT
undergo alcohol treatment for at least 6 months to reduce or eliminate offender's dependency on alcohol. Needs offender's consent / co-operation to participate

8 DRUG REHABILITATION
includes drug treatment and testing. Can be imposed as part of community sentence or custodial sentence. Can also order review of this requirement – must do so if order for more than 12 months. Court must be satisfied offender is dependent on or has propensity to misuse controlled drug and may benefit from treatment. Needs offender's consent / co-operation to participate

7 RESIDENCE **to reside at specified place for specified period**

OR : Not to do: Court can order offender :
Not to leave a set address / not to go to certain places / not to do a certain activity.

---

8 CURFEW **not to leave fixed address between set times for set period.** For max. of 6 months, for 2-12 hours in one day. Often enforced by electronic tagging. Court should avoid imposing conditions which interfere with offender's work, education, religious beliefs.

9 PROHIBITED ACTIVITY
refrain from participating in certain activities, for period of time
e.g. forbid offender from contacting certain person or participating in specified activities **or from possessing, using, carrying a firearm.**

10 EXCLUSION **to stay away from** specified places at specified times. E.g. the pub; also aimed at stalkers.

For adults and all young offenders under 25 years
  ➢ **Attendance Centre**
  Visit specified centre for minimum of 3 hours per visit for period fixed by court.

For adults only
  • **Compensation -** pay sum of money to victim. Max £5,000 in Mags court
  • **Restitution -**   to return the stolen property to the victim
  • **Deprivation and forfeiture -** take the property used to commit the crime e.g the car of drink-driving offender.

For Young offenders only
  • **Supervision -** placed under supervision of probation officer Youth Offending Team
  • **Action plan –** supervision plus requirements, e.g. exclusion, attendance centre.
  • **Reparation –** offender pay back victim or society in some way. Eg repair damage, letter of apology

And remember:
  o **Increasing emphasis upon reparation to victim and parental responsibility**

....

CUSTODIAL SENTENCE - LOSS OF LIBERTY

S152 CJA 2003 –   only if "so serious" that neither a fine nor a community sentence could be justified in the circumstances.

Custodial sentence
FOR **YOUNG OFFENDERS:**
In Young Offenders Institution
*Young offenders are **10 – 20** years incl.*

detention @ Her Majesty's pleasure   *["life sentence"]*
  o **10-17 years for murder**
  o S90 PCCSA
  o judge recommend min. years before release, Lord Chief Justice sets tariff

Detention and Training Order   *["term of years sentence"]*
  o **12-20 yrs**
  o **Term of between 4-24 months** [either 4, 6, 8, 10, 12, 18 or 24 months]
  o Under 15 yrs only if persistent offender
  o 10-12 yrs only if Home Secretary orders this sentence
  o **Extended detention**
    o **10-17 for serious crimes**
    o 10-13 yrs if offence max 14 yrs sentence or indecent assault on women
    o 14-17 yrs if death by dangerous driving or careless as under influence drugs/alcohol

Note: 10-13 included since 1994 when court unable to give custodial sentence to 13 year old boy who raped 12 year old girl

THE DURATION & TYPE DEPENDS UPON AGE OF YOUNG OFFENDER & SERIOUSNESS OF OFFENCE

Custodial sentence
FOR **ADULTS:**
- loss of liberty -
In Prison, for LIFE or TERM OF YEARS
Term of years sentence can be extended or suspended!

S152 CJA 2003 – only if "so serious" that neither a fine nor a community sentence could be justified in the circumstances.

LIFE SENTENCE:

This sentence is for life, however with date set for when parole can be considered – hence "life does not necessarily mean life"

MANDATORY
For murder, repeat rape or gbh
i.e. judge no choice, must give life sentence

DISCRETIONARY
For serious offences such as manslaughter, rape, gbh – judges choice/discretion whether to give life sentence or not. **CJA 2003 states:**

- o **Actual life** should be given for those convicted of the most serious and heinous crimes: e.g. multiple murderers, child killers, terrorist murderers
- o **30 years** - as starting point for murders of police / prison officers or murders with sexual or racial or religious motives
- o **15 years** - as starting point for other murders
- o once these minimum terms have expired the Parole Board will consider suitability for release from prison.

TERM OF YEARS – set number of years

Term of years for violent or sexual crimes Or if defendant refuses a Com. Sentence

SUSPENDED where offender does not go to prison, unless commit further offence, for period of up to 2yrs in Crown court and up to / 6 months in Magistrates court. If commit offence this sentence is "activated".

EXTENDED term of years, when served term the offender is at liberty on licence for max 10 yrs for sex crime and 5 yrs for violent crime.

Home detention curfew early release on condition curfew included

Since CJA 2003, <u>two new sentences</u> when less than 12 months is the term given:

- o <u>**Custody Plus**</u> Offender spends max of 3 months in prison, remainder (of at least 6 months) under supervision in community
- o <u>**Intermittent Custody**</u> Offender serves sentence intermittently: returning to prison at night or weekend. Idea to enable offenders to continue employment / education / family ties to reduce risk of offending.

<u>Also, Dangerous Offenders – CJA 2003,</u>:
A new scheme for sentencing dangerous adults – if committed specified sexual / violent offence and assessed as dangerous – release is discretion of Parole Board – new power to keep in for indeterminate period: allowing state to hold offenders
in prison for longer than is required by gravity of their offence, because they pose a danger to society if released.

Discharge

- **For offender of any age**
- Commonly issued for first-time offender who has committed minor crime
- 2 types, given where character of offender and nature of offence are such that punishment is NOT appropriate

Either:

A **Conditional** discharge   no sentence on condition defendant does not re-offend for a set period   (max 3 years).   If does re-offend, will then receive sentence for the offence originally discharged, plus new offence.

OR:

an **unconditional** discharge where no penalty is imposed. E.g. if defendant is "technically guilty" but morally blameless. Or believe time served "on remand" (as bail denied) is sufficient punishment.

Summary of TYPES of sentence - **actual punishment**

FINE

- **Monetary punishment**
- To reflect seriousness of offence
- Taking into account: offender's means / age of young offenders
- However Magistrates' court is limited to imposing a maximum of £5,000 fine.

COMMUNITY SENTENCE

- **Offender remains at liberty**
- **Requires offenders co-operation to agree to do / not do certain activities**
- The range of activities (requirements) available depends upon age of offender
- Increasing emphasis upon reparation to victim and parental responsibility
- Many activities are aimed at changing the offender's behaviour (rehabilitation)

CUSTODIAL SENTENCE

- **Loss of liberty**
- In prison (for adults); in Young Offenders Institution (for young offenders, 10-20 years old incl.)
- **Either for life** (with recommended time before parole can be considered); as a mandatory or discretionary sentence
- **Or for a set duration (term),** which can be **extended** or **suspended**
- However, offender rarely serves full sentence – released early "on licence"

DISCHARGE

- **No actual punishment**
- **Usually on condition** that offender does not commit a further offence within a set period of time. If he/she does re-offend then a sentence will be issued for the discharged offence.

The type of sentence (and duration) is decided by the Judge in Crown court trials and by the magistrate in Magistrates' court trials *(unless it is a triable-either-way offence which was sent to Crown court for sentencing).*

Murder and repeat offences of gbh / rape carry a mandatory life sentence. For all other offences it is the discretion of the judge/magistrate which sentence to impose. However, their discretion is increasingly being limited by legislation.

SENTENCE	ADVANTAGES	DISADVANTAGES
CUSTODIAL	o **Protects the public** from dangerous criminals, but only for time they are in prison - & offenders rarely serve the full duration. o Intermittent Custody & Custody Plus sentences enable balance between punishment , protection of public and the needs of the offender: enabling offender to retain family ties / job. However, some view this as "soft option" o Reflects Government's policy of being "tough on crime"	o Prisons are **overcrowded, expensive** to run and conditions often poor. o Punish the innocent as well : **families suffer** o Prisons do **not offer opportunity to rehabilitate**, due to overcrowding & lack of funds – often said to be "university of crime"! – 50% of prisoners re-offend within 2 years of release. o **Many who are in prison should be elsewhere** : mentally ill, trivial shoplifters, fine defaulters … 8% of male, 15% of female prisoners have previously been admitted to psychiatric hospital
COMMUNITY SENTENCE	o Provides a **flexible approach** to sentencing – a wide range of requirements to choose from - to fit the **punishment and rehabilitation need to individual offenders** : from treatment to unpaid work – yet enable offender to remain in society : work / family ties. However, curfew and exclusion restrict offenders movements & provide protection for the public . o Many offenders say that supervision was **useful** – talking about their problems to member of probation service.	o The requirements are often viewed as a **"soft option"** o Electronic tagging to monitor whether offender is abiding by curfew requirement is expensive & degrading – yet less degrading than being in prison. o Statistics show that **approx 44% re-offend within 2 years** : rehabilitation does not address problems in society / background, merely assumes behaviour can be altered. o Critics argue the emphasis upon this sentence is merely to address problem of overcrowding in prisons
FINE	o Statistically fines have the **lowest re-offending rates** – however this could be due to the type of offender receiving fines o **Source of income** for the criminal justice system o Can be combined with community sentence & custodial sentence.	o **Many offenders fail to pay** their fine – in May 2006 this totalled £130 million. However, a national enforcement service & detachment of earnings orders should go some way to addressing this problem o The re-introduction of unit fines could lead to **unfair** high fines for relatively minor offences merely in attempt to create fairness: similar impact of fine on all offenders.

AIMS OF SENTENCING - theories of WHY punish

AIMS of sentencing	*Types of sentence which achieve the aim*
### *Retribution* **Look at offence only** Punishment for having committed a crime • Punish **because offender committed an offence** : "just desserts" for offender's actions **"an eye for an eye, a tooth for a tooth, a life for a life.."** • Idea of set tariff – set sentence for each offence, regardless of circumstances. Contains element of revenge • Foremost theory behind CJA 2003 and PCCSA 2000 – sentence proportionate to the crime committed.	**Adult custodial sentences** **Curfew requirement** **Fine** R v Billam (1986) Court of Appeal guideline for set sentences for rape
### *Rehabilitation* **look at offender only** [opposite to retribution] To change behaviour of offender • Penalty imposed **to reform offenders behaviour** – rehabilitate into society • Individualised sentences. • Main aim for young offenders • Aim behind most community sentence requirements • Forward looking aim, however based on assumption that problem is with offender – what if problem is society?	• **Young offender custodial sentences** • **Majority of requirements for community sentence:** e.g. unpaid work / supervision / drug and alcohol treatment
### *Deterrence* **fear of punishment.** To deter from re-offending/offending • Fear of harsh punishment in order to deter: • **Individual** from committing crime again • **General** public from committing any crime – but requires public to know of the harsh sentence • Probably the least effective and least fair aim of sentencing, yet still find harsh, disproportionate sentences ordered: e.g. football hooliganism / mobile phone theft • This aim is in direct conflict with aim of rehabilitation	• **As for retribution above, but harsher sentence** • **Football hooliganism:** R v Whitton (1985) given life sentence, reduced to 3 years on appeal – to deter • **Mobile phone theft**, Lord Chief Justice increased sentence from 6 months to 3 years as deterrence – 1 million thefts in 2002
### *Protection of Public* [incapacitation] • **Protect the public by removing offender from areas of society** • Legal right of society to protect itself from persistent and dangerous offenders stated in DPP v Ottewell (1968). • This aim is reflected in parts of CJA 2003 and PCCSA 2000 – 'only impose custodial sentence where offence so serious … and only such a sentence would be adequate to protect society."	• **custodial sentences** prevent the offender from committing crime – whilst in prison / young offender institute • **curfew and exclusion requirements** for Community Sentence protect the public by limiting where / when the offender can be in public places.
### *Reparation* **compensate victim / society** • focus upon the effect of the crime • Under S130 Powers of Criminal Courts (Sentencing) Act 2000, court under duty to give reasons if they do not make a compensation order.	• **Community sentence requirements of:** • Compensate victim by: Return stolen articles / apology letter / repair damage • Compensate society by: Unpaid work where work on community project e.g. paint school buildings

Discretion: how judge/magistrate decides sentence

The courts have all four TYPES of sentence available to them:
Custodial / community sentence / fine / discharge

However, the judge / magistrate must take account of the following:

1. The COURT they are in

- Magistrates' court   limited to 12 month custodial sentence and max of £5,000 fine
- Crown court   limited to maximum stated in the statute for the offence
                          e.g. Theft Act 1968 states maximum of 7 years custodial

2. SENTENCING GUIDELINES

- The Sentencing Guidelines Council was set up by CJA 2003.
- Issues guidelines on sentencing – to promote consistency in sentencing
- Is advised by the Sentencing Advisory Panel
- Takes account of cost and effectiveness of sentences
- E.g. **reduction in sentence for a guilty plea.**   Up to one-third if plead guilty at first reasonable opportunity – then sliding scale up to one-tenth reduction for changing plea to guilty after trial has started.

3. The OFFENCE and the OFFENDER

- persistent offenders minimum sentences for repeat of certain offences:
  - e.g.   drug trafficking - S110 PCC(S)A 2000 minimum sentence of at least 7 years custodial
  - e.g.   domestic burglary – S111 PCC(S)A 2000 minimum sentence of 3 years [for third conviction.]

- the offence   whether fine is proportionate to the crime committed; or
                      whether community sentence is more appropriate; or
                      whether offence so serious only custodial sentence is justified.

- <u>Mitigating</u> and <u>aggravating</u> factors
  - **Looking at:**
    - **the nature and seriousness of the offence; and**
    - **the circumstances**
  - **In order to decide whether to increase / reduce sentence**

  e.g. **consider factors of:**
  - offence committed whilst on bail for another offence
  - amount of money / injury / damage caused / violence involved
  - offender's first offence [criminal record]
  - drugs involved
  - racial motivation
  - age of offender
  - was offender in position of trust – which he abused
  - financial status of offender
    - **Aggravating factors** – those which indicate **increase in seriousness** of offence
      - Hence should receive _**harsher sentence**_ than originally considered
    - **Mitigating factors** – those which indicate **decrease in seriousness** of offence
      - Hence should receive _**lighter sentence**_ than originally considered

4. the AIM of sentencing   Whether sentence achieves that aim; and which aim is offender likely to respond to – with reference to pre-sentence report

Types of sentences

1   Frodo Baggins aged 51 has been convicted at the Shire Magistrates' Court of the theft of a ring. Describe the range of sentences available to the magistrates to impose on him
OCR AS Level Law, June 2003, Q2

2   Describe the sentences available to the courts for young offenders.
OCR AS Level Law, June 2004, Q3

Aims of sentencing ... & types / & mitigating, aggravating factors

1   (a)   Briefly describe the different aims of sentencing.

        (b)   Illustrate the ways in which different sentences may be used to support different aims of sentencing.
OCR AS Level Law, June 2001, Q2

2   Phoebe (aged 30), with no previous convictions for burglary has been found guilty of robbery.
Chandler (aged 32) with no previous convictions has pleaded guilty to minor theft.

      Consider how the aims of sentencing and other factors will be taken into account when sentencing these two offenders.
OCR AS Level Law, January 2004, Q7

New specification specimen question: [see examples on pages 50, 63, 73, 78, 99]

1   (a)   Describe the sentences available for adult offenders. [18]

        (b)   Discuss the advantages and disadvantages of custodial sentences. [9]

OCR AS Level Law, Q1 specimen paper G141QP [total 30 marks; AO3 worth 3]

Criminal APPEALS

Function of an appeal:
- o **To protect the def. from miscarriage of justice**
  - ▪ *process by which judge reconsiders aspects of original trial, with power to alter the outcome (conviction/sentence).*
- o **To allow uniform development of the law**

Need to know, and be able to compare & contrast: **Appeal routes:**
For both prosecution and defence / From trial at either Magistrates' court or Crown court.
APPEAL ROUTE DEPENDS UPON COURT TRIAL HELD IN & WHO IS APPEALING

**Appeal route
from Magistrates'
Court trial.**

> ### QBD of High Court.
> 2/3 High Court judges
> Power to:
> Confirm or reverse conviction, or find guilty
> of a lesser charge. OR send case back to
> Mags' court to implement their decision on
> point of law.

APPEAL BY WAY OF CASE STATED

                                        [prosecution and defence agree facts of case]
- • **By DEFENCE & PROSECUTION**
- • **As of right**   [not need permission for appeal]
- • **Against conviction**
- • **On point of law** [claim error in law makes conviction "unsafe"]
- • [possible further appeal to House of Lords – need leave & only on point of law of general public importance]

> ### Magistrates' Court
> ### TRIAL

- • **By DEFENCE ONLY**
- • As of right
- • **Against conviction** (if def. pleaded not guilty at trial) **&/or sentence**
- • **On point of law &/or fact**
- • Possible further appeal to QBD (as stated above)
- •

> ### Crown Court.
> Judge & 2 magistrates hear appeal.
> Power to:
> Confirm / **increase** or decrease the **sentence**.
> Confirm or reverse conviction – OR find guilty
> of lesser charge.

> *In 1994: 22,600 appeals
> by defence to Crown court
> - of which 43% were
> successful!*

- a.   All appeals from Magistrates' court are "as of right" – automatically allowed if apply.
- b.   **Unusually, prosecution can appeal an acquittal** from Magistrates' court – but only on the ground of error of point of law.
- c.   **Unusually, the sentence of the defendant can be increased** by Crown court.

1.   The magistrates can rectify their error: under S142 MCA 1980 (as amended) power to retry case before different bench of magistrates, if is in the interests of justice to do so.
2.   Criminal Cases Review Commission can refer cases from Mags to Crown court for appeal.

Appeal from Crown Court trial.

> ## Court of Appeal *(criminal division)*
>
> **If defence appeal:**
> Confirm or decrease the sentence- **[not increase]**
> Confirm or reverse conviction – OR find guilty of lesser charge OR order a retrial under CJA 1988
> **If Att. General appeal unduly lenient sentence:** the court can increase the sentence.
> **If Att. General refers an acquittal, on point of law** the court cannot alter the acquittal, but can clarify the law – set precedent

> **[possible further appeal to House of Lords** – need leave, & only on point of law of general public importance] This is available for both prosecution and defence. .

By DEFENCE
Need leave
Against sentence &/or conviction
On point of law &/or fact
[defence must file notice of appeal within 28 days]

Attorney General (for PROSECUTION)
1. **appeal against unduly lenient sentence** under S36 CJA 1972 **(need leave)**
2. **Make reference on point of law re: defendant' acquittal.** Under S36 CJA 1988
[note that there is generally no right of appeal for the prosecution against an acquittal, in order to prevent oppressive use of the criminal justice system]

Crown court **TRIAL**

By PROSECUTION ONLY
- **Against conviction [defendant's acquittal]**
- **If have conviction for "jury nobbling"**
- (threats / bribery of jury or witness at trial)
- [very rare]

> ## High court. – very rare.
>
> Power under Criminal Procedure and Investigations Act 1996 to order a retrial – acquittal is arguably due to outside pressure and not reached on basis of evidence at trial.

LEAVE:
- All appeals **from trial in Crown court require leave** [permission.]
- **This is either obtained in the form of a certificate from the trial judge OR permission from a single judge in the court they wish to appeal to.**
- Since CAA 1995 there is now only one ground (legal reason) for granting leave (allowing an appeal): **If the judge thinks the conviction "is unsafe"** . i.e – that the trial outcome (conviction/sentence) is questionable – (due to the appeal grounds of error in fact &/or law)

NEW EVIDENCE:
If new evidence is the consideration for the appeal, the **judge must consider whether such evidence:**
1. Is capable of belief
2. Afford the ground for appeal
3. Is admissible in court; and
4. Why it was not produced at trial.

COMPARISON OF APPEAL ROUTES:

By <u>DEFENCE</u>:

* From **magistrates'** court the **appeal is "as of right"**
* From **crown** court the defence need **leave** (permission) before they can have an appeal.
  * *In 2003, 7,451 applications for leave were considered but only 2.218 were granted – approx. 30%*
  * *In 1994, there were 22,600 appeals from the magistrates' court, of which 43% were successful.*
* From **magistrates'** court the defence may have their **sentence increased** (by Crown court) however the **sentence cannot be increased on appeal by defence from Crown court trial.**

* **Defence can appeal against both conviction &/or sentence, on grounds of errors of fact &/or law from both courts. However, extra hurdle of obtaining leave from Crown court.**

By <u>PROSECUTION</u>:

* **Re: CONVICTION:**
  * **From magistrates'** court the prosecution can appeal against a defendant's acquittal [to QBD but only on ground of error in law / procedure];
  * however **generally there is no right of appeal from an acquittal at Crown court trial.** Unless a conviction for "jury nobbling" when a retrial can be ordered [interference with jury or witness questions whether verdict due to interference or evidence in court].

* **Re: SENTENCE:**
  * **From magistrates'** court the prosecution cannot appeal the sentence;
  * however from Crown court trial the Attorney General may appeal against an **"unduly lenient"** sentence – the Court of Appeal could then increase the sentence.
    * In 2003 there were 249 such appeals.
    * e.g. *case of Luan Plakici in 2004 whose trial custodial sentence of 10 years was increased to 23 years by the Court of Appeal: Guilty of kidnapping girls for sex and living off their prostitution.*

Ensure that you know the differences between when prosecution & defence can appeal against conviction &/or sentence – and to which court they appeal – and differences in powers of appeal court to alter the original trial outcome : conviction / sentence

Exam Questions on criminal appeals

1 Describe the rights of the defence to appeal from both the Magistrates' Court and the Crown Court.
   OCR AS Level Law, January 2005, Q3

2 Describe the rights of **both** the prosecution **and** the defence to appeal from the **Crown Court.** Include further appeals to the House of Lords.
   OCR AS Level Law, January 2006, Q3

New specification specimen question: [see examples on pages 50, 63, 73, 78, 99]
The question, if on the paper, will be in the new format – example below:
   (a) *Describe (appeal routes)*   *.... For 18 marks ... AO1*
   (b) *Discuss (comment upon appeal routes)* *.... For 9 marks AO2*
        [total 30 marks; AO3 worth 3]

Civil Disputes

- **Claimant** claims **DEFENDANT** has breached his civil law rights
  - e.g. breach of contract / been negligent
- and asks court to award **REMEDY**
  - [usually **damages** (monetary compensation for loss suffered); but also injunctions, decrees of specific performance & rectification.]
- Claimant starts claim, must prove "civil wrong" on **balance of probabilities**
- **Private matter** – can settle at any time, [only approx 5% end in court]

Jurisdiction   of High court and County court
Which court to start civil claim in? ......

Both courts have unlimited civil jurisdiction – able hear all civil cases
Noting that High court has 3 divisions, each specialising in different areas of civil law:

QBD	contract, tort …
Family	family law e.g. divorce, adoption
Chancery	Equity based law e.g. Wills and probate, trusts …

However,

┌─── **3 factors** display difference in jurisdiction / may affect choice of court:-

1 **EXCLUSIVE JURISDICTION:**
Of High: defamation / fatal accidents / claims against police
Of County: Personal Injury for less than £50,000
Must go to that court, regardless of value and content of claim

2 **VALUE OF CLAIM:**   [if not within exclusive jurisdiction]
Amount in damages being claimed
CLSA '90:   more than £50,000 must go High court : County limit £50K
Small claims: 0-5k must use small claims procedure
                   – only available County court
If straightforward case, 5-15K should use **FAST TRACK**,
                   - only available at County court

3 **CONTENT OF CLAIM:** [of claims for over £5,000 – i.e. over small claims limit]
i.e. facts and law in claim
COMPLEX   content should go HIGH court
High court able hear all complex cases over £5K
General rule: If straightforward content, 25K – 50K is claimants choice of court

PROCEDURE [in starting claim / civil case]

1. Claimant issues claim - pay fee
2. Court sends claim to defendant, requiring reply within 14 days
3. Defendant can:
   - acknowledge claim and lodge defence – dispute; or
   - Admit and settle; or
   - Do nothing – then Claimant gets judgment in default,
     defendant can still defend if present to court good reasons why "did nothing" – why he did not reply

> Once case is defended, the judge will assess case and can transfer: hence, although claimant starts the case in one court the judge may transfer it to the other – looking at content / value.

Track systems / procedures at court: small claims/fast track/ multi track

small claims
- available in county court – since 1973
- idea that informal, quicker, cheaper, simpler procedure
- District judge – more active
- No legal aid – idea "litigant in person"
        lawyers allowed but discouraged
- Increase public confidence
- legal system not only accessible to rich and powerful

> **BUT**   (small claims)
> - small claims not necessarily simple claims
> - May be imbalance between parties – especially since increased limit from £1,000 to £5,000 [AJA 1999]
> - Still delays and Increased fees [AJA 1999]
> - No legal aid yet could face lawyer

Fast track
since April 1999 [AJA] - Lord
        Woolf recommendations
Faster, cheaper procedure
Straightforward cases - £5,000 to £15,000
Restrict discovery
Trial approx 3 hours, max. one day
Fixed timetable and start claim to trial approx
30 weeks
Expert evidence limited to written reports

Multi track
cases claiming above £15,000 or less if complex case
Individual case management by judge
Tailor-made directions according to the needs of the case
Often conference first:
- identify issues
- Procedural directions
- Set timetable, which can only alter with judge's permission

For both multi and fast track, judge can fine lawyers if deviate from timetable
These reforms to procedure are aimed at reducing cost and delay in civil courts.

Problems with civil courts   *- before AJA 1999*

COST   Too expensive mainly due to lawyers costs and delays. Often the cost exceeded the amount being claimed. Further, the risk of having to pay the other party's legal fees if lose case and costs awarded by the judge. Costs put people off going to court: reduce access to justice.

DELAYS   Could be up to 3 years from incident to case being heard in County court, and up to 5 years for High court. These delays increase costs and cause undue stress for parties to case.

COMPLEXITY   The complex legal terminology and forms requiring use of lawyers, which increases costs.

PRESSURE TO SETTLE   The costs and delays arguably cause pressure to settle the claim out of court – which may not give rise to a fair settlement – depends upon equality of bargaining power between the parties!

TECHNICAL CASES   Often the dispute resolves not around issues of law but around technical issues: e.g. building disputes, employment disputes - then court may not be the most suitable forum – experts in the field of dispute would be needed as witnesses in court case. Hence increasing use of ADR – where experts in field decide the dispute.

LACK OF ENFORCEMENT   Despite going to court to achieve a legally binding decision if one party does not adhere to the decision then another trip to court is needed to legally enforce the courts decision – it is not automatically enforceable!

Created in order to eliminate the above problems with courts: cost / delay / complexity …

Lord Woolf recommendations:

[most of which were enacted by Parliament in AJA 1999 & Civil Procedure Rules]
in order to:
- "create a new landscape for civil justice" &
- "simpler, more accessible, more flexible system."

Lord Woolf recommended introducing:
- o **case management** [for judges]
- o **Fast and multi track procedures**
- o **More encouragement of use of ADR, by judges**
- o **Increase small claims limit**
- o **To reduce legal terminology in forms**

Main aim is to encourage settlement, and if this fails to ensure cases progress as quickly and economically as possible. To create a system which is "just in the results it delivers" and "fair in the way it treats litigants"- which is used as a last resort.

Fast and multi tracks are explained above. ADR is explained below.
Case management: a new, more "active" role for judges to ensure costs and delays are kept to a minimum. Identify issues at an early stage to encourage settlement; set timetables and encourage use of ADR. Judge can fine lawyers if not keep to timetables. Active role to ensure proceedings run to time and efficiently – to ensure openness and cooperation between the parties instead of "trial by combat" (in true sense abolished in 1819); *although it is still an* **adversarial system**.

Reforms: AJA 1999 and

[details in **Civil Procedure Rules which came into force in April 1999**]
- New fast and multi track procedure   (*as explained under jurisdiction on opposite page*)
- Increased small claims limit to £5,000   (*as explained under jurisdiction on opposite page*)
- Greater encouragement of use of ADR
- Make forms/process easier to understand: eg claim form replaces writ for High court and summons for County court.

Criticism of reform - by Michael Zander:

- Whether track system does reduce costs
- Whether judges can take on new role of case managers – cost of training
- Delays - noting worst delays are in personal injury cases and reforms unlikely affect these
- Whether increased limit in small claims and increased encouragement to settle or use form of ADR instead of court - is merely increasing the pressure to settle.
- Described reforms as *"using a sledge hammer to crack a nut"*

Comment on reform:

- Volume of litigation has fallen since April 1999 – the rate of settlement has increased.
- Judges are applying timetables strictly – *as seen in Vinos v Marks and Spencer plc (2000) where court struck out claim which was served on the defendant 9 days late.*
- Does seem to be some reduction in time between incident and court case.

However,
- Increased fees in making a claim [initial increase in cost]
- Still problems in enforcing a judgment
- The reduction in litigation could be due to other factors: e.g. increased use of conditional fee agreements / withdrawal of legal aid from personal injury claims …

A.D.R   *Alternative Dispute Resolution*

- Where to go, other than court, to resolve dispute in civil law
- **Designed to be cheaper, quicker, and less formal than court**
- Where use of lawyers discouraged – hence **general rule is no legal funding available**
- Often court is not best option – especially technical cases [judge is legal expert]
- However, many cases encouraged go to ADR in order to reduce number of cases in civil courts – **"rough and ready justice"?**
- Any method other than court will be a form of ADR e.g. Parties **negotiating** amongst themselves, in private. This is the quickest and cheapest method of settling a dispute.

Go to: **Arbitration** OR **Conciliation** OR **Mediation [or negotiation]**

Similarities:

- Both parties must **agree to choose ADR** instead of civil court
- Put their case in front of a **neutral third party** (in court this is a judge)
- The procedure is **less formal** than court, and often cheaper.

Differences:

- **Only in Arbitration will the third party impose a legally binding decision**
    - o i.e. the decision (called an award) is enforceable at court, if one party does not adhere to the decision. [note, this is a similarity between court and arbitration.]
- **In Conciliation and Mediation the parties are encouraged to reach the decision themselves** with the help of the neutral third party. Their decision is not legally binding – hence not enforceable in court. In Conciliation the third party plays a more active role, suggesting a solution. NOTE: **Negotiation** is the only form where only the parties attend: no third party.

Arbitration:

- 1 or more Arbitrators – usually expert in field of dispute (or legal expert)

- **Parties choose:**
  - Arbitrator
  - Date, time and place
  - Procedure: whether oral or written presentations by parties

- Arbitrators decision:
  - Is called an **award**
  - **Is legally binding**

- Parties must both agree to use arbitration instead of court
    However, may have done so, albeit unknowingly, if signed document containing
    a **Scott v Avery clause**: agree use arbitration if dispute in future.
    E.g. in building / holiday contracts.
These written agreements to arbitration are governed by Arbitration Act 1996

Arbitration often used in Commercial disputes between businesses OR consumer claims.

Example:
ABTA – Association of British Travel Agents -offers conciliation between tour operators and consumers. If this fails have special arbitration scheme – where about half cases succeed but now always winning amount claimed.

Advantages:

Greater flexibility for parties:
- Expert in field saves expense of calling expert witness
- **Parties can choose** date, time & place convenient to them
- **More informal** and relaxed hearing which is less antagonistic then adversarial court procedure
- **Private hearing** – no publicity
- **Quicker than court**
- Can **enforce** award (decision) at court

Disadvantages:

Especially if parties not of equal bargaining strength:
- Legal aid **not** available
- **Arbitrator's fees often expensive** (end up same cost as court)
- Dispute **may involve legal issue** (arbitrator usually not lawyer)
- **Limited rights of appeal** – award (decision) usually final
- **Delays** can be same as for court case.

All forms of ADR have the aim of avoiding the time and cost and "battle atmosphere" which a court case involves. Judges now must encourage ADR as part of their "case management" duties. Judges can "stay" court proceedings (put on hold) until a form of ADR has been tried. The Court of Appeal has shown it is prepared to punish parties who refuse to try ADR, by not making an order for costs, even if the court case is successful. However, parties still display a reluctance to use ADR.

Mediation:

- o Neutral third party – mediator
- o **Helps parties reach a solution** (compromise)
- o Consult with each party and help find common ground
- o Can take different forms – parties choose method
- o Only suitable if parties will cooperate
- o Often private individuals where relationship needs to be sustained after dispute settled
- o e.g. families, neighbours
- o Are commercial mediation services
- o e.g. Centre for Dispute resolution in London
- o BUT for all mediation is **no guarantee parties will reach a solution**
- o AND if do reach solution, <u>it is not legally binding – not enforceable in court.</u>

Conciliation:

[a more active form of mediation]

- o Neutral third party – conciliator
- o **Plays more active role than mediator –**
- o **Suggest a solution**.
- o But still parties themselves who reach solution
- o <u>Like mediation, the solution is not legally binding.</u>
- o Like mediation, this process requires parties to cooperate
- o e.g. for **employment disputes use ACAS** – Advisory Conciliation and Arbitration Service. Attempt to resolve dispute without going to tribunal – has trained conciliators. Over half employment claims are settled this way – yet argued unfair pressure on employee to settle

Remember: *Mediation / Conciliation / Negotiation are only suitable if the parties are willing to cooperate – if some chance they will reach a solution / resolve the dispute themselves.*

Negotiation:

Like Mediation and Conciliation (above), in negotiation the parties reach agreement themselves; which is not legally binding. In contrast, there is no third party involved in the negotiation. This is the quickest and cheapest method of resolving a dispute. The negotiations may take place through solicitor instructed by each party.

Comparison of ADR and COURT

A.D.R	COURT
CHEAPER & QUICKER	MORE EXPENSIVE & LONGER
Although arbitration could be as expensive as going to court – pay for arbitrator – & no legal funding is available for ADR.	cost of legal fees is very high, often more than the claim is for & increased court fees. Delays in waiting court date / procedure – which in turn increase costs.
IN PRIVATE	IN PUBLIC
Advantage for businesses wishing to keep information given private	Details made known to anyone who attends – e.g. reporter / business competitor
INFORMAL	ADVERSARIAL
Enables parties to maintain relationship business / neighbour / family relationships	involves winner / loser – process pits parties E.g. parties against one another / difficult to maintain relationship following court

ADR MAY ALSO BE MORE SUITABLE: expert in area of dispute in Arbitration resolves dispute, whereas called as witness in court as legal expert (judge) resolves dispute.
BUT REMEMBER ONLY ARBITRATION AND COURT PROVIDE LEGALLY BINDING DECISIONS

Exam Questions on A.D.R

1   Describe the different methods of Alternative Dispute Resolution available to deal
    with civil cases. Do not include tribunals.
                    OCR AS Level Law, January 2006, Q4

2   Discuss the advantages of using alternative methods of dispute resolution rather than
    using the courts.
                    OCR AS Level Law, January 2004, Q6

New specification specimen question: [see examples on pages 50, 63, 78, 99]

    (a)   Describe the different methods of Alternative Dispute Resolution available to
          deal with civil disputes.   [18]

    (b)   Discuss the advantages and disadvantages of using Alternative Dispute
          Resolution. [9]

          OCR AS Level Law, Q4 specimen paper G141QP [total 30 marks; AO3 worth 3

Civil Appeals

Function:	**To correct wrong decisions at first instance**
	To enable law to evolve

Since reforms introduced under AJA 1999 / Civil Procedure Rules:
 ➤ Either party can apply for an appeal
 ➤ On grounds of error in fact or law or procedure
 ➤ Require "leave" – permission for appeal
 ➤ From either first instant judge or judge in the court appealing to
 ➤ Decision for granting appeal is based upon prospect for success or some compelling reason for an
    appeal
 ➤ Possible second appeals will be the decision of the Court of Appeal
 ➤ Appeal hearing is usually a review of the first instant decision, rather than a full rehearing of the case.

From County Court:
Fast track cases (& small claims) heard by district judge   appeal to **circuit judge**
Fast track cases (& small claims) heard by circuit judge   appeal to **High Court judge**
All Multi track cases   appeal to **Court of Appeal (civil division)**

From High Court:
All cases   appeal to **Court of Appeal (civil division)**
       Or   **"leapfrog" straight to the House of Lords**, under Administration of Justice Act
                1969, for appeals which involve a point of law of public importance, concerning
                interpretation of legislation or binding precedent.

From Magistrates' Court:
Family proceedings   appeal to the High Court (family division)
Licensing matters   appeal to the Crown Court
Judicial review   appeal to the High Court (QBD division)

 • **There is a possible further appeal from the Court of Appeal to the House of Lords.**
 • **This requires "leave" (permission)**
 • only on points of law of public importance.
 • Leave is difficult to obtain
 • The House of Lords usually only hears approx. 55 civil law cases a year

o *You need to know:*
   o Qualification; Appointment and Selection and Training; / Role (what they do)

o *Need to be able to comment upon:*
   o **Independence**
      o That judiciary need to be independent in order to effectively fulfil their role.
      o i.e. free from pressure!
   o **Criticism**
      o That judiciary are not representative of society:
      o Said to be : "elderly, white, upper-class and male" …. & out of touch with society"
      o that we do not have a "career" judiciary NOR   a single "Ministry of Justice"

<u>Note</u> that most of above comments / evaluation are linked with role of judiciary
<u>Remember</u> that judges are either termed: Superior or Inferior - depending upon court in which they sit (work) – and difference in appointment and tenure

* *

<u>Qualifications:</u>   title, court sit in and qualifications needed.

	Superior judges			**Inferior judges**		
Title	**Law Lords** [Lords of Appeal in Ordinary]	**Lord Justices of Appeal**	**Puisne judges** [High court judges]	Circuit judge	District judge	Recorder [part-tine judge]
Court	**House Of Lords**	**Court Of Appeal**	**High Court**	**Crown** & **County** Courts	**County** court – small claims & **Magistrates'** court	usually in **Crown** court but some in **County** court
How Qualify	**15** years rights of audience in superior court or held high judicial office for **2** years	**10** years rights of audience in superior court or currently a High court judge	**10** years rights of audience in superior court or currently a Circuit judge (for **2** years)	Rights of audience: <u>For Crown</u>: **10** years in Crown court <u>For County</u>: **7** years in County court or currently a District judge or recorder (for **3** years)	**7** years general rights of audience	**10** years general rights of audience

SUPERIOR JUDGES

* **appointed by Monarch, on advice of Prime Minister, after short-listed by Lord Chancellor** from those **selected by Judical Appointments Commission**

* by **invitation only**

* Used to be following **"secret soundings"** : [discussions with other superior judges!]

      ○ with exception of High Court judges – adverts

"Secret soundings" and "invitation" argued as perpetuating male dominance & select political views – not merely merit of judge.
Note not all of those "invited" accept – difference in "passive" role of judge from "active" role of advocate in court – as well as drop in wage for top barrister to become judge.

- Judges used to be recruited only from the Bar - Barristers,
- However, CLSA 1990 widened the entry to include solicitor advocates, and academic lawyers. Hence Greater cross-section of society able to apply to be a judge.
- Lord Chancellor is key figure in appointment of ALL judges.
- All judges must retire at 70 years of age – since 1993

- **Security Tenure:**
- **"whilst of good behaviour" can remain a judge** – only removed from office by Monarch for "misbehaviour", after petition by both Houses.

Such security of job is essential to ensure independence of Judiciary, but few removed.

Only once – Irish judge removed for misappropriation of funds – Rarely a judge put under pressure to resign e.g. Harman J – High Court Judge: 20 month delay in giving judgment / voted worst HC Judge in unofficial poll by Bar! - **No ability to remove incapable superior judge!**

INFERIOR JUDGES

* **position advertised**

* **Judicial Appointment Commission select / interview**

* **Security of Tenure "misbehaviour and capacity"** hence less secure than for superior judges.– i.e. **two grounds for removal, by Lord Chancellor, but still rare** … but

      ○ *1983 Judge Bruce Campbell dismissed after being caught smuggling substantial amounts of cigarettes and whisky into the country in his private yacht!.*

      ○ *In 1994, Ld C said drink-driving, a conviction for any offence involving violence, dishonesty or immorality … would be regarded as "misbehaviour" however in 1999 Judge Victor Hall was allowed to keep his job following conviction for drink driving, with condition he not sit on motoring offence cases.*

Main criticism: **mostly MALE of certain POLITICAL views:** [specifically chosen or those available?]
- Politically appointed Lord Chancellor involved in all selection/appointment
- Judicial Appointments Commission - approx 10 commissioners, most non-lawyers, who can <u>investigate</u> appointment procedure but <u>do not themselves make appointments</u>.
- "Secret sounding" mean unable to discover why candidates appointed, or not
- Despite adverts/applications for inferior judges and despite CLSA 1990 enabling wider choice of candidates – still seems Judges heavily recruited from BAR [barristers].

Further criticism: that once appointed often not use specialism of candidate, e.g. Charles J in 1998 was appointed a judge in Family Division despite his experience being as highly-regarded Chancery lawyer!

Reform: Constitutional Reform Act 2005 changed appointment procedure –now carried out by **new Judicial Appointments Commission** – [JAC] members of judges / legal profession who should appoint **solely on merit** and consult with Lord Chancellor – **greatly reducing Lord Chancellor's powers to appoint** – however still involved in formal appointment of superior judges – but JAC has enabled transparency and consistency in appointment process – on merit. This should combat criticism of political influence in appointment and selection by politically appointed Lord Chancellor.   New Judicial Commission began during 2006.

To **adjudicate** on **disputes** in a **fair and unbiased way,** applying the legal rules of this county.
To **supervise** and **control proceedings,** and make decision at the end**.**

At FIRST INSTANCE (trial)

<u>CIVIL</u>: (a) Judge must **decide liability** – [decision based upon facts as applied to civil law]
Decide whether claimant has proven, on balance of probabilities, that defendant has breached claimant's civil law rights; and

(b) if liable, **decide upon the amount of damages** to award the claimant as compensation for loss suffered; or other appropriate remedy. Damages payable by the defendant.

o Judge is **case manager** (see p69), deciding track, hold preliminary hearings to decide issues.
o Judge in QBD of High court may hear cases for Judicial Review.
o **Decide questions of law.**

<u>CRIMINAL</u>: In Crown court:

(a) judge **summarises the facts and law to the jury**; and explain that they must vote guilty if they believe the prosecution has proven guilt, beyond a reasonable doubt.

(b) If guilty then it is the **judge who decides upon the sentence** (punishment)

NOTE: if is District judge in Magistrates' court, he/she decides both conviction and sentencing issues. [no jury]

ON APPEAL

o Judge decides whether to **grant leave** (allow appeal) – if leave is required
o Judge decides whether **to dismiss appeal; or alter the trial outcome** (conviction / sentence for criminal & liability/remedy for civil) **& Decide questions / interpretation of law.**

Remember, the judge is not re-hearing the whole trial, merely arguments for appeal.

[see pages 64-66 for further detail on appeals]

TRAINING:

Carried out by Judicial Studies Board, since 1979

Existing judges – courses

- **New judges – 3 weeks practical training**:
    o Rules of evidence / communication skills / empathy & sensitivity / ethnic
    o Awareness / prison visit
- **Human Awareness training** since 1993 - e.g. racial awareness course
- **Equal Treatment Bench Book**, since 1990, given to all judges, idea stop prejudice against: homosexuals / disabled / litigant in person / domestic violence
    o YET:
- **Very little training – but improving**
- *Often judge appointed to court in which little or no experience!*
- *Need to focus on the change in role from practising legal professional to judge.:*
    o *e.g. R v Gunning (1980) judge asked def. 165 questions!*
    o *E.g. R v Bentley (1988) CA overturned conviction partly based upon the judges bias towards prosecution when summing up to jury.*

NOTE: **No career judiciary in our ELS –**

In other countries students choose to train/qualify as judge after gaining law academic qualifications. Hence find younger judges with greater training in skills needed to be an effective judge.. However are all civil servants hence closely linked with Government which questions their independence. In our English legal system judges are appointed from among practising lawyers / academic lawyers – superior judges restricted to those with higher-court rights of audience.

Judges should be **fair and unbiased**; protect liberty of the individual from abuse of power by the executive (government) In order to do this judges **need to be free from outside pressure**.

Doctrine of Separation of Powers – by Montesquieu: [constitutional theory]
- primary functions (arms) of state
- all 3 should be independent and separate bodies; [to safeguard liberty of citizens]
- which check and balance power of others – therefore power not concentrated in one area
- *I.e. individuals should not be members of more than one arm / function – enable independence*

The 3 "arms" of state:

The *Legislature*	law-making arm	Parliament
The *Executive*	administer the law	Government / cabinet
The *Judiciary*	**apply the law**	Judges

Independence of Judiciary:

Judges should be FREE FROM BIAS:
Yet they are not totally free from political pressure; and **often said to be Pro-establishment**
As seen in "GCHQ" case (1984) HL upheld ministers right to withdraw right to trade union membership from civil servants at intelligence headquarters. Seen as anti-trade union.
However, many cases show judges being Anti-establishment:
as seen in DPP v Hutchinson (1990) HL ruled in favour of Greenham Common women - held minister exceeded powers by framing bylaw to prevent access to common land. Also in, A and another v Secretary of State for the Home Department (2004) HL held Anti-Terrorism, Crime and Security Act 2001 breach Human Rights Act 1988 which forced the Government to change the law.
Judges should also be impartial: excuse themselves from the case if an interest in the the dispute / a connection to the parties involved- as clearly *stated by HL in Pinochet case in 1998.*

INDEPENDENT FROM the Legislature:
Judges **not allowed to be members of Parliament. But 12 sit in House of Lords!**
and take part in the legislative process of the House. Generally they do not take part in legislative debates but confine themselves to technical questions of law rather than political issues
This should be rectified with new Supreme Court being proposed – no longer a House of Lords court but Supreme court which not at Westminster. – no connection to legislative House.

INDEPENDENT FROM the Executive:
- Judges cannot be dismissed by government – **Security of tenure.**
However, can be pressure by government:
  - *For Judges to resign* – although is rare (see e.g. on p74)
  - *In terms of appointment and promotion of judiciary*
- Judges not paid by government **– paid by separate fund**
- Judges **not appointed by government** – but politically appointed Lord Chancellor selects all superior judges and input in appointment of all inferior judges. However new Judicial Appointments Commission should address this issue.

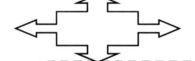

JUDGES SHOULD BE:
FAIR and UNBIASED, and
PROTECT LIBERTY OF INDIVIDUAL FROM ABUSE OF POWER BY STATE:
Need to be **free from all outside pressure** – able to challenge government decisions [*which can do in Judicial Review cases*] and immune from being sued by parties to the case
[*yet immunity is decreasing…*]

Judges are said to be "Old, Upper-class, white and male": *judiciary*

The issue here is:
- **Whether the above statement is true; and**
- **If so, whether this is due to the selection process or the "pool" of available candidates.**

There are many comments which can be made with regard to age, gender, education of judiciary today – examples follow:

- **Only 15% of Judiciary are female**
  - but is improving – one female in HL.
  - However, women tend not to apply for inferior judicial post as readily as men.
- **Black, ethnic judges in the minority**
  - 1st Black High Court Judge, and a woman, appointed 2004
  - 25% of those currently taking Law degrees are non-white origin [– improving.]
- **Most judges are over 40 years old**
  - Currently youngest judge appointed was 39 years old
  - most are mid 20's before finish qualifying as legal professional!
  - Tend to be 50's before appointed as superior judge, and retire at 70.
  - In early 2002 youngest High Court judge was 47 and all but one of Lords of Appeal
  - were over 60.
- **Most are upper-class publicly educated**
  - *some ¾ still come from upper to middle-class background,*
  - *and from independent schools or Oxbridge –*
  - *from 1997 to 1999, 85 judges were appointed, of which **73%** had been to public school,, most to Oxbridge – [survey by magazine Labour Research]*
  - *but is improving as more people can afford the education – however, may alter now pay for University!*

The majority of judges are still male, white, in their 50's, middle-classed and publicly educated !

Main criticisms:
Not representative of society; and "out of touch" with society; and Pro-establishment
  - *Harman J "who is Gazza?"; and Wild J "A girl who hitchhikes at night is "asking for it"*
  - *[see p69 for case examples of pro and anti establishment]*

The judiciary would certainly be more representative if it included more women, more members of minority ethnic groups, more working class people and more young people – however given the length and cost of training to become a solicitor or a barrister, it would seem the above quote is to a large extent reflective of those who are qualified to and wish to become judges!

In other words: at the moment, because of social history, most of the best people to do the job are rather elderly white males from upper middle-class backgrounds.

Exam Questions on the Judiciary

1 Discuss how far judges are independent. *OCR AS Level Law, June 2005, Q5*

2 Describe the qualification, selection and appointment of judges. *OCR AS Level Law, June 2004, Q1*

3 (a) Explain how judges are appointed and how both the selection and training of judges have been affected by the Courts and Legal Services Act 1990 and other subsequent changes.
  (b) Discuss the view that judges are "old, out of touch and mainly white and male."
    OCR AS Level Law, June 2002, Q1

4 Discuss whether or not the most appropriate people are chosen as judges.
    OCR AS Level Law, January 2005, Q6

New specification specimen question: [see examples on pages 50, 63, 73, 99]
  (a) Outline the theory of separation of powers, illustrating your answer with examples [18]
  (b) Discuss the ways in which judges' independence is maintained. [9]
    OCR AS Level Law, Q5 specimen paper G141QP [total 30 marks; AO3 worth 3

o *You need to know: -*
  - o Qualification; Appointment and Selection and Training; / Role (what they do)
  - o Regulation and complaints procedures.

o *Need to be able to comment upon:*
  - o **Changes to role**
    - o The loss of monopolies for each profession / changes to rights of audience
    - o Whether current training needs to be reformed to reflect current role
    - o Difficulties facing students wishing to enter either of the legal professions.
  - o **Regulation and complaints procedures**.

* *

Qualification and training:

Both go through the same three stages:
Academic / vocational / practical

However, the vocational and practical stages are different [– to reflect different roles.]

ENSURE YOU CAN EXPLAIN THE <u>PROCESS</u> / <u>STAGES</u>:-

SOLICITOR   BARRISTER

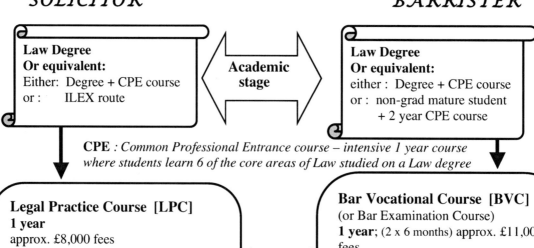

Law Degree
Or equivalent:
Either: Degree + CPE course
or :   ILEX route

Academic stage

Law Degree
Or equivalent:
either : Degree + CPE course
or : non-grad mature student
         + 2 year CPE course

CPE : *Common Professional Entrance course – intensive 1 year course*
where students learn 6 of the core areas of Law studied on a Law degree

Legal Practice Course [LPC]
1 year
approx. £8,000 fees
College of Law; or University offering course.
[some centres offer "City LPC" – specialisation]
Practical skills of advocacy, interviewing and negotiation. **Legal and procedural knowledge** in main areas of solicitor's work:

Vocational stage

Bar Vocational Course [BVC]
(or Bar Examination Course)
1 year; (2 x 6 months) approx. £11,000 fees
1 of 4 Inns of Court or 1 of 8 Universities offering course.
Practical skills of advocacy, interviewing and negotiation; writing opinions, rules of evidence.
(Litigation: rules and procedure)
Legal research.
Membership of 1 of 4 **Inns of Court**
Dine there 12 times [or weekend course] <u>QUALIFIED AS BARRISTER</u>

Training Contract

2 years "on the job training" usually in **solicitor's firm**
paid a **salary**
cover 4 areas under supervision of senior solicitor.
Admitted as qualified solicitor
["on the roll"]
plus further exams organised by the Law Society

Practical stage

Pupillage

1 year "on the job training", in **chambers**
small salary [half that of trainee solicitor]
shadow, then on own in court.
Plus further exams organised by The Bar Council.

Difficulties facing students wishing to enter either of the legal professions

o **EXPENSE**

o Tuition fees payable for all stages & need to cover living expenses
o University up to approx. £9,000 tuition fees for 3 years
o LPC approx. £8,000, and BVC approx. £11,000 for tuition fees.
o Small salary whilst undertake training contract and even smaller whilst undertake pupillage
o No grants available

o HOWEVER:
o Some solicitor firms pay cost of LPC for student
o Some chambers subsidise or guarantee minimum income to tenants
o Bar Council offers scholarship to pupils
o Students more likely to be middle class with parental support, & still large debts

o **TIME IT TAKES TO QUALIFY**
o Quickest route for is 6 years to become solicitor, and 5 years to end of pupillage as a barrister.

o **COMPETITION**
o High competition for places: many more candidates than are places, for all stages.
  o At university
  o On LPC and BVC
  o For training contract and pupillage.

o **ABILITIES NEEDED TO QUALIFY:**
  o Academic ability
  o Practical approach to problems
  o Communication skills

Anyone with real ability is not stopped from qualifying, although may be discouraged by expense and the time it takes to qualify and earn a decent salary. Currently the legal professions contain approx. equal numbers of men and women, but an under-representation of ethnic minorities.

Role - (what they do):

Solicitors:
Approx 75,000 in private practice

Role depends upon size of firm:
Small town / village or City firm
• **deal with public directly**
• "legal GP", dealing with:
  o conveyancing (buy/sell houses)
  o divorce – family matters
  o wills
  o consumer issues

• **advice and representation for civil and criminal matters** (litigation):
  o eg civil claims for accident / employment / consumers.
• Larger firms tend towards specialising in different areas – commercial in city firms
• Some solicitors work in Law centres, or for the CPS or other Government department, or in private industry.

Barristers:
Approx. 10,000 in chambers

• **Representation in court**
• Preparing opinions
• Drafting pleadings
Most specialise:
  • Eg. Common law, family or chancery work
  • Or more narrowly in:
    Eg. Libel, taxation, criminal.
Note: approx. 2/3 in London
    approx. 3,000 work employed
      eg for CPS, Companies.
Since 2004 barristers have direct access to client, with exception of family and criminal proceedings & asylum/immigration cases.
(– no need go through solicitor – but likely to have little impact as barristers not authorized to handle client money, nor to prepare cases – hence will still need a solicitor in most cases.)

Traditionally the roles were quite separate, with barrister (specialist advocate) representing the client in court – when hired by the solicitor, who deals with the client directly; undertaking all legal matters, not just those involving litigation (court cases). **In past few years these roles have been changing** – "fusing": as today both barristers and solicitors can represent clients in all courts.

Changing role of the Legal Profession:
(1) Due to <u>loss of monopolies</u> in certain areas of work:

<u>Conveyancing</u>
– solicitors lost monopoly
This areas of work was opened up to
Banks and Building Societies by
CLSA 1990 – today probate work
can be carried out by banks and even
"Tesco Law"

<u>Rights of audience</u>   **– barristers lost monopoly**
Barristers: All courts
Solicitors:
Traditionally able to advocate in lower courts:
[Mags courts / County courts / tribunals and some
crown court work]
CLSA 1990: **with "certificate of Advocacy"**
                  able to advocate in all courts
AJA 1999:   LPC : all new solicitors can advocate in all
                  courts, but still need further training in order to
                  exercise this right.

(2) But, with increased rights of audience has come decreased <u>immunities:</u>

<u>Negligence:</u> standard of work – (**today will be liable if below standard**)
- **<u>Advocacy work:</u> no longer immune from claim of negligence**
  - For both solicitors & barristers, since *Hall v Simons (2000)* HL :
    i. [HL overruled earlier case of Rondel v Worsley (1969)]
    ii. Duty to conduct case with reasonable care and skill – if not can be sued for loss suffered by client
- **<u>Work carried out outside court:</u> never had immunity.**
  - Barrister: Saif Ali v Sydney Mitchell & Co (1980)
  - Solicitor: Griffiths v Dawson (1993)
  - Both have duty to conduct case with reasonable care and skill (as above)

<u>Contract:</u> (promise to do work)
solicitors always had contractual duty with the client: directly deal with client :
liable in contract: be sued if fail to carry out the work / solicitor sue client if they not pay fees.
This will now apply to all barristers who are directly instructed by the client.

(3) Still retained Q.C - Queen's Counsel

QC – "taking silk" - "elite advocates"

10 years practice as barrister or solicitor advocate – able to apply to become a QC
Approx 10% of BAR are QC's
Take the more complicated, high profile cases – and command higher fees (for their expertise)

Office of Fair Trading (OFT) recommended abolishing this position, stating it did not benefit the
public: not necessarily offer a better service, with no monitoring of quality and high costs to hire.
In 2004, the new system of appointment was outlined: [as agreed by Lord Chancellor, Bar
Council and Law Society] : a new selection panel, chaired by a non-lawyer but with lawyers
on the panel would interview and select candidates to appoint. Candidates can bring
references. This replaces the previous, much criticised, and secretive appointment by Lord
Chancellor (following invitation to apply) – and retains the stated advantages of having QC's:
- A known brand which public recognise as mark of quality of advocacy
- Provides a resource for public enquiries.
- Provides recognisable specialists for complex cases.

Today, still separate professions:

Solicitors are predominantly "legal general practitioners" in high street firms, and "commercial practitioners" in city firms. Barristers are still largely specialists (advocates); but the difference is lessening. Barristers are also "losing work" in criminal litigation due to the government setting up "in-house" lawyers working for the CPS.

(4) Arguably we have gained all the benefits of "fusion", without incurring the disadvantages of total "fusion":

CLSA 1990 and AJA 1999 have addressed the **main advantages** stated in the **"fusion debate"**
All preparation and court advocacy can now be carried out by one legal professional:
o **reduce cost to client**
- o only pay for one lawyer if solicitor happy to advocate in court (or instruct barrister direct)
- o reduced cost due to:
- o greater efficiency
- o no duplication of work

o **greater continuity for client**
- o client often more at ease when only deal with one lawyer
- o increase public confidence in the legal system

Yet, have **not incurred the main disadvantages of total fusion:**
Not lost : [the following would be lost if total fusion occurred]
- **cab rank rule**: for barristers
  - o must accept client if barrister is available / case is within their area of law & reasonable fee
  - o (solicitors can decide not to act for client)
- **availability of second opinion by Bar**
  - o solicitor still able get second opinion from barrister (opinion)
- **availability of specialist skills of advocacy**
  - o barristers still mainly advocate – retain honed skills.
  - o Solicitors do not have to advocate, but now able to in all courts.

(5) Summary of benefit to clients from changes listed above:

- **greater choice of advocates** for representing case in court.
- **Reduced costs** if solicitor prepares case and represents client in court – especially as many cases the solicitor prepares in the High street firm turn on the facts as opposed to complex issues of law ("minor cases")
- **Ability to hire barrister direct** (without solicitor) **advantage for certain clients** who can prepare the case themselves but require advocate for court, eg businesses with "in-house" lawyers, accountants, legal centres and CAB preparing case for clients.
- **Still able to hire barrister** in complex cases- retain specialist advocate.
- Solicitor **still able to get second opinion from barrister**
- **Training is more practically based** – greater emphasis on skills on LPC and BVC .
- And, **quality improved** through greater controls over traineeships / pupillage
- **Training now continues past qualification** – to ensure standards maintained.
- New LPC courses suited to City firms – specialism.

Solicitors   **Professional body: the <u>Law Society</u>**
Barristers   **Professional body: the <u>Bar Council</u>**

Regulation and complaints:

Main criticism:
That the professional body's cannot carry out two conflicting roles effectively:
a) **represent interests of its members AND**
b) **deal with complaints against its members**.

> **Professional Body:**
> * Maintain standards of profession
> * Regulate education and training
> * Develop and promote work of the profession.
> * & deal with complaints against members of their profession.

Client has 3 stages to the complaints procedure:
1. **The solicitor's firm / barrister's chambers;**
2. **The professional body :** Law Society (solicitors) / Bar Council (barristers);
3. **The Legal Service Ombudsman** – independent but government appointed.

Law Society *Professional body for solicitors* In response to growing
criticism, set up separate body to examine complaints against solicitors:
OSS: Office for Supervision of solicitors set up in 1966.
Consists of committee of 25 members: 10 members of public and 15 members who are solicitors (of which 10 are also members of the Law Society Council). The Director also sits on Law Society Management Board.
* **Although is separate body, with lay members, it is not totally independent of the Law Society and is still funded by the Law Society.**
* **Delays occur:** backlog of 17,000 complaints by 1999
* Still prone to interpret rules of professional behaviour in favour of solicitors
* Still only able to award compensation up to £1,000 to client.
Very serious complaints are referred to the Disciplinary Tribunal (see below)

Bar Council
Professional body for barristers
Since 1997, client's complaint is considered by: a non-lawyer:
Complaints Commissioner who can order compensation up to £200 or dismiss claim or send claim to:
PCC: Professional Conduct & Complaints Committee who can discipline the barrister, award higher compensation to client or dismiss claim. Serious claims of misconduct are referred to the Disciplinary Tribunal.
Delays occur – but 50% completed within 3 months in 2005.

Disciplinary Tribunal
Complaints about solicitors or barristers can be referred (by OSS and Complaints Commissioner) to tribunal. A statutory body composed of lawyers and
lay people, with disciplinary powers over legal professionals accused of professional misconduct.
Tribunal has the power to:
* **Reprimand** the solicitor / barrister
* **Fine**
* **Strike solicitor off the roll / disbar the barrister**

LSO: The Legal Service Ombudsman – – set up in 1991
To oversee the complaints procedure – (ensure no bias by professional bodies towards their members.) Current LSO is Zahida Manzoor, CBE (plus 35 office staff and investigators)
Examines the handling of complaints by the professional bodies, on behalf of members of the public.
checks complaint addressed, and within a reasonable time.
Not investigate the original complaint.
Client must contact LSO within 3 months of the complaint being dealt with by the professional bodies.
Can recommend professional body reconsider complaint / make payment to client / formerly criticise.
As general rule, professional bodies follow the LSO recommendations.
Oct 2003. LSO had 231 cases, and completed 80% within 3 months of receiving them.

Summary

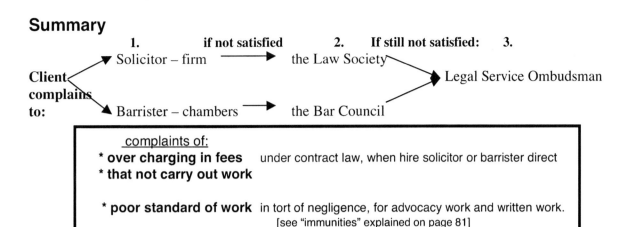

1.   if not satisfied   2.   If still not satisfied: 3.

Client complains to:
→ Solicitor – firm → the Law Society
→ Barrister – chambers → the Bar Council
→ Legal Service Ombudsman

---

 complaints of:
* **over charging in fees**   under contract law, when hire solicitor or barrister direct
* **that not carry out work**

* **poor standard of work**   in tort of negligence, for advocacy work and written work.
[see "immunities" explained on page 81]

Still criticism:

Of self-regulation by professional bodies: (insufficient independence)

Despite each body separating their regulation and complaints functions & including non-lawyers:
* creation of OSS, Office for supervision of solicitors (with non-lawyers and solicitors)
* Creation of position of Complaints Commissioner and PCC (non-lawyers & barristers on committee).

CLEMENTI REVIEW:

By David Clementi; report published in December 2004
with following recommendations:
* **Create new legal regulator:** *Legal Services Board*
  Responsible for overseeing regulation of the legal profession
* **Create new complaints body**: *the Office for Legal Complaints*,
  to handle all complaints from consumers of legal services (clients)

REPORT recommendations were published in a White Paper in 2005;
and still **currently at the Bill stage of legislation** – Legal Services Bill 2006/07

> *Griffiths v Dawson (1993)* is case illustration of *negligence of solicitor:* failing to make correct application in divorce proceedings. Solicitors *ordered to pay client £21,000 compensation* for financial loss suffered due to negligence of solicitors.

> The Law Society investigated a complaint against a solicitor, *Glanville Davies,* and found he had acted properly. However, in 1986 the High Court held that *Glanville Davies, had overcharged a client by £131,000.* Following this decision the Law Society realised it needed a more independent complaints procedure.

> **It is not only the client who can sue:**
> Other people affected by lawyers negligence:
> As seen in *White v Jones (1995)* intended beneficiaries under a will successfully sued their father's solicitor for the £9,000 inheritance each that they lost because the **solicitor failed to draw up the will**, as instructed to do so by their father in July '86, before their father died Sept. '86.

Exam Questions on the Legal Profession

1 Describe the qualification and training needed to become a barrister.
   OCR AS Level Law, June 2004, Q2

2 Describe the different ways in which unsatisfactory work and behaviour by a barrister and a solicitor can be dealt with.   *OCR AS Level Law, June 2003, Q3*

3 Discuss whether the training of solicitors needs to be reformed.
   OCR AS Level Law, June 2004, Q6

New specification question: [see examples on pages 50, 63, 73, 78, 99]
(a)   **Describe the training of barristers and solicitors [18]**
(b)   **Discuss the disadvantages of the current system of training barristers and solicitors.   [9]**   *[total 30 marks; AO3 worth]*
   OCR AS Level Law, G141, June 2007, Q5

○ *You need to know:*
  - ○ Qualification; Appointment and Selection and Training; / Role (what they do)
○ *Need to be able to comment upon:*
  - ○ Whether we have cross-representation of society as magistrates and juries
  - ○ To what extent juries are randomly selected / how to improve selection
  - ○ Advantages and disadvantages of using lay people in decision-making process.

* *

- **'Lay'' meaning not legally qualified.**
- **Tradition of using non-legally qualified people in the decision-making process in our courts.** This is cornerstone of our English legal system:
  - ○ **Fundamental right to trial "by one's peers"**
  - ○ Therefore, we need a cross-representation of society to be magistrates and juries.
  - ○ [then justice is not only done, but seen to be done.]

JURY	MAGISTRATE
<u>Selection:</u> **Randomly selected From electoral register**	<u>Selection:</u> **Selected for their qualities**

<u>Requirements:</u>
AND: if selected must be:
<ul><li>**Aged 18-70**</li><li>**resident in UK, least 5 years since age 13 years**</li></ul>AND: if selected must **NOT** be:
<ul><li>**DISQUALIFIED:**<ul><li>○ serious criminal conviction</li><li>○ those on bail</li></ul></li><li>**EXCUSED:**<ul><li>○ military personnel</li></ul></li><li>**iNELIGIBLE:**<ul><li>○ those with mental illness</li></ul></li></ul>[since 2003, reduction in those able to be excused jury duty – but can apply to judge for discretionary excusal (state good reason why cannot attend jury service).
(see notes on next page]
 	
Once selected, at court: some jury members may be withdrawn – unable to sit as member of jury:
  <u>*Challenges:*</u>
  Whole jury – for bias
  Individual juror – for cause – eg knows defendant or witness *[see notes on next page]*
	<u>Requirements:</u>
	a) Formal requirements:
	Age: 18 – 65 years
	Residence: Within 15 miles of commission area of the court.
	b) Character requirements:
	[1988 Lord Chancellor guidelines] <u>6 key qualities</u>
	good character / understanding & communication / social awareness / maturity & sound temperament / **sound judgement / commitment & reliability**.
	
	iNELIGIBLE:
	<ul><li>Those with serious criminal record</li><li>Member of forces</li><li>Those whose work incompatible</li><li>Eg police officer … and their relatives.</li></ul>**LOCAL ADVISORY COMMITTEES:**
	<ul><li>**Advertise vacancies** for magistrates</li><li>Must consider anyone who applies or is nominated (eg by trade union …)</li><li>Members of committee:<ul><li>○ 12, current and ex-magistrates</li></ul></li><li>**2 interviews –** one to assess attitudes, one to practical based on sentencing – **To check above requirements are met / ability.**</li><li>**submit names to Lord Chancellor**</li></ul>

Central Juror Summoning Bureau sends **summons** to individuals selected from electoral register – with date/time to attend court; and form to return confirming individual does not fall into any of disqualified, ineligible or excused categories. **Jury at court chosen by random ballot by the clerk of the court.**	Appointed by **Dept. Constitutional Affairs** <ul><li>Appoints from list from advisory committee</li><li>idea to create panel of magistrates that is representative of all aspects of society</li><li>approx. 1500 appointed a year.</li></ul>

whether true representation of society is appointed.

Juries:

Not everyone in society is eligible to be summonsed for jury duty. For those who are it is said to be their civic duty. Hence, a total representation of society is not achieved.

'POOL' of available people **LIMITED TO:**
- *Only those who are on electoral register*
- *Who fulfil the age and residence requirement*
- *And who are not disqualified, excused or ineligible.*

The "pool" **COULD BE WIDENED IF:**
- **Replace random selection from electoral register with random selection from those able to vote** - many are not on register e.g. homeless, many young people & ethnic minorities.
- **Lower minimum & maximum age but** would they be capable to fulfil role?
- **Select jury to ensure balance of sex/race**

> **Recent reform:** CJA 2003 abolished category of "excusal as of right": Today, certain professionals e.g. doctors, M.P's, legal professionals cannot now be **automatically excused** if they are summonsed for jury duty; but may still be excused at judges discretion if they can give good reason – this reform does mean more of society are **able to sit on a jury panel.** *However, this has led to a judge sitting as a juror – in June 2004!*

Further possible improvements include:
- ➤ **Closer checks on whether jurors are disqualified or ineligible.** Many are still end up serving on jury panel
- ➤ **Set minimum education standards.** Many jurors are not able to follow proceedings and legal terminology
- ➤ **These suggestions ("further possible improvements") are to improve ability of jury to fulfil role, but would again reduce the likelihood of having a cross-representation of society on the jury panel.**

Magistrates:

- The **aim of the selection process** is to create a panel that is representative of all aspects of society : **A balanced mix of age, race, political views, occupations**.

- However, currently **magistrates do not represent all aspects of society – but it is unlikely that they ever could:** given that they need to commit to giving up their time, unpaid, to sit in court for a minimum of 26 times a year, and attend training: **not everyone can afford to do so; even if they wanted to.**

- **Therefore, the comment that magistrates are : "middle-classed, middle-minded & middle-aged".** It would seem that these are the people who can afford and wish to apply to be a magistrate. Despite the concern that selection is by all magistracy membership of Advisory Committees

Of the 29,000 current magistrates:
- Most are **45-65** years old
- The majority support the **conservative** party
- The majority are professionals; managers
- **Approx. 40% are retired.**
- **The young and working class are under-represented.**

However:
- **There are approximately equal men and women**
- **With fair representation of ethnic minorities (in relation to percentage of population)**

Challenges of jury panel just before they are sworn in at court: By prosecution & defence:
- (a) **against entire jury for biased or unrepresentative selection;** as seen in 1993: the "Romford" jury were excused because 9 out of the 12 came from Romford, with 2 living in the same street.
- (b) **Against an individual juror, for cause:** must give valid reason e.g. juror is disqualified or knows, (is related to) the defendant or a witness.
- (c) **By prosecution only:** "stand by " juror : a right which enables such jurors to be put to the end of the list of potential jurors at court, and only used if there are not enough other jurors. This right should be used sparingly.

All such challenges go against the idea of random selection., However, even the current process of random selection does not necessarily provide a cross-section of society. (as seen in the "Romford" jury case above)
NOTE: There is no right to "hand-pick" the jury: R v Ford (1989) held no right to a multi-racial jury.

Role: what they do

Role - Jury   [judge of fact]
Summonsed – usually sit once in a lifetime, if at all. [Role is to bring their viewpoint to the case – as lay person.]

Criminal:
TRIAL: AT CROWN COURT
Decide issue of conviction:
For **indictable offences**. (serious offences, eg murder, manslaughter, rape & triable-either-way offences being tried in Crown court). Jury must rely upon their common sense, to weigh up the evidence presented at trial and decide which were the true facts. Then apply these facts to the law – as explained to them by the judge – to **reach a decision as to whether the defendant is guilty** (beyond a reasonable doubt) **or innocent.**
[the judge decides upon sentence].
jury of 12 people

Civil:
High and County courts
Only in less than 1% of civil cases:
Cases involving Defamation; false imprisonment; malicious prosecution; and fraud.
(1)   **Decide issue of liability** of
              defendant:
Whether they believe claimant has proved, on balance of probabilities that defendant breached claimants civil law rights. [see top of page 20] AND
(2)   if liable; **decide the amount of**
              damages to be awarded.
Jury of 12 in High court.
Jury of 8 in County court.

Coroners' court:
Jury when death occurred in following situations:
• Prison;
• police custody or by police officer in execution of his duty;
• industrial accident;
• incidents involving public, e.g. tragic accident of Marchioness in the Thames – public heath & safety issues.

Role - Magistrate
Sit regularly, as volunteers
In Magistrates' court; for a minimum of 26 days / year; on bench of 2/3.

Criminal: (clerk advises them on law)
1   **TRIAL:**
•   **Decide issue of conviction**: innocence/guilt
•   **issue sentence** of those found/plead guilty
•   **For all summary offence and most triable-either-way offences**. Some 97% of all criminal cases.
2   **PRE-TRIAL:**   (see page 45)
•   **EAH (Early Administration Hearing) for all criminal cases** – including indictable offences: - decide issues of bail, reports, legal funding.
•   **Plea before Venue / Mode of Trial / Committal hearings for Triable-either-way offences**, to decide which court for trial.
3   **POLICE MATTERS**: issue warrants, extend police detention.
4   **APPEAL:** sit in Crown court, with judge, to hear appeals from magistrates' court. (see page 64)

[Plus specially trained magistrates sit in **Youth Court**, private trial within **Magistrates' court –** try cases involving offenders aged 10 – 17 inclusive. However, not those prosecuted for murder, manslaughter, rape, death by dangerous driving; who are tried in the Crown court – along with offenders 14years plus prosecuted for a serious arrestable offence which carries a possible custodial sentence of at least 14 years.]

Civil:
In **Family court** (branch of Magistrates' court).- specially nominated/trained magistrates **hear certain family law cases**, eg proceedings under the Childrens Act 1989.
Enforce debts:
Eg. owed for utilities of gas/electric/water
         Non-payment of TV licence
Admin. Duties: granting licences eg for sale of alcohol

Ordinary men and women, with no legal qualifications, carry out all of the above duties unpaid on a part-time basis.

• Magistrates deal with the less serious criminal offences, but these account for 97% of all criminal cases.
• Juries deal with approx. 1% of criminal cases, but these are the serious offences.
• Magistrates decide both stages of the criminal trial: conviction & sentencing, whereas juries only decide the conviction issue.
• Both have limited role in civil cases, although in civil the jury decides both liability and damages.

Advantages & Disadvantages of using lay people:

Advantages:

- **Closer to a cross-representation of society than the judiciary**
  - **Fundamental right to be "tried by one's peers"**
  - Hence often more able to relate to defendant's world
  - Have local knowledge
  - But also able to express society's disapproval
- **Use common sense to decide verdict**
  - **"Jury Equity":** can base decision on their idea of "fairness". They do not have to follow precedent.
  - This is also seen as a disadvantage (see below)
- **Sit as a group, so that prejudices can be cancelled out.**
- **Justice is seen to be done: public confidence**
- **Cheaper than using judiciary**
  - all only paid expenses.
  - **Estimate of £100 million a year to replace lay magistrates with judges.**

[Note: can find District judge in magistrates court, but more often is bench of 2/3 lay magistrates.]

> **Use of local knowledge**:
> In *Paul v DPP (1989)* magistrates used their own knowledge of an area being heavily populated residential in deciding that the defendant was "likely to cause a nuisance" by picking up a prostitute in his car in that area.

> **Jury equity**: seen in *Ponting's case (1984)* even though judge ruled there was no defence the jury refused to convict the defendant of leaking information about the governments involvement in the sinking of the Belgrano in the Falklands war [contrary to the Official Secrets Act 1911.] Jury believed that it was in the public's interest to know this information

Disadvantages:

- **Neither jury nor magistrates are a true cross-representation of society:**
  - *Magistrates said to be "middle-class, middle-aged, middle-minded"*
  - *Not everyone can be summonsed for jury service,*
  - *and of those not all actually serve.   [see page 78]*
- **Jury no choice if summonsed** (is one's **civic duty**)
  - *Which disrupts their lives,*
  - *their objection to being on jury may affect their participation/verdict.*
- **Jury deliberates in secret: unknown if bias / prejudice occur**
  - *& not have to give reason for their decision.*
- **Juries are said to acquit too many people**
- **Juries often have difficulty understanding/following complex legal issues**
  - *Especially in civil cases: hence reduction in use of juries in civil cases*
  - *current criticism is that juries are still used for long and complex fraud cases.*
  - *Current criticism that juries award too high amount of damages in civil cases.*
- **Juries can return what is said to be a "perverse decision"**
- **Media coverage may influence the jury**   [e.g. Rosemary West's trial]
- **Magistrates are often more likely to convict than jury:**
  - *Magistrates' said to be **"case hardened"** often hearing same minor offences*
  - *And **"pro-prosecution".***
- **Magistrates are inconsistent in their sentencing:**
  - ***Sentencing varies from bench to bench – a "geographical lottery":***
  - *1990 Liberty study showed twice as many defendants were sent to prison in Greater Manchester than in neighbouring Merseyside.*
  - *1995 Home Office Study found major difference in sentences for same type of offence:*
  - *70% went to prison in West Derbyshire for driving whilst disqualifies, compared with 0% in neighbouring Cirencester.*
- **Limited training for magistrates**, training varies from bench to bench
  - *There is no national training programme*
  - ***and yet magistrates carry out many and varied roles*** [see opposite page]
- **No legal qualification for either magistrates or jury**
  - However, law and procedure is explained to jury by the judge, and to magistrates by the clerk of the court (Magistrates' clerk is a solicitor or barrister of at least 5 years qualification)

> **Jury Equity:** often acquit according to their conscience and *"there but for the grace of god go I"*. As argued when created new offence of causing death by dangerous driving due to lack of jury convictions for manslaughter in this situation

> **Decisions based on irrelevant factors:** *In R v Young (1995)* four of the jurors are said to have **used a ouija board** to contact one of the defendant's alleged victims to find out whether the defendant had killed them,.

This is not intended to turn Magistrates into lawyers but **to give them an understanding of their duties.** The **focus is upon court procedure and the practice and theory of sentencing.**

- Their training is supervised the Magistrates Committee of the Judicial Studies Board and carried out locally by the clerk of the court.
- Guidelines for training are found in the Magistrates National Training Initiative 2004 (MNTI2)

- <u>The training can be summarised as follows:</u>

    i.   Training **focus is upon skills** of managing oneself / making decisions / working as a team member and role of a Magistrate

    ii. There is an **initial induction course** on appointment concerning workshops and observation of court procedure.

    iii. Continuing with **further 7 short training sessions** at local court

    iv. Each magistrate keeps a **Personal Development Log** of their progress and regularly meets with **mentor** who is an experienced Magistrate

AND, have a **Magistrates' Clerk** to advise as to law & procedure:

- Magistrates' only sit if they have a legally qualified clerk to assist them.
- Clerk must be a solicitor or barrister of at least 5 years
- Under S28(3) Justices of Peace Act 1979 are there to:
- Advise as to law and procedure - [not decision making]
- In R v Eccles Justices (1992) the convictions were quashed (overturned on appeal) due to the participation of the clerk in the magistrate's decision to convict.
- The powers of the clerk are increasing. Today can issue warrants / extend bail.

However:
- o Training of magistrates **seems to vary from region to region** ["geographical lottery']
- o Seems to **depend upon time and enthusiasm of the clerk**
- o **With inconsistencies in sentencing** [see page 80 "disadvantages" section]

Alternatives – to using lay people:
- ➢ A judge
- ➢ A panel of judges
- ➢ Judge and lay people

However, all of the above would result in:
(1)   A vast increase of cost for the government:
- o **Estimate of £100 million a year to replace lay magistrates with judges**.
(2)   An end to our fundamental right to be "tried by our peer's"
- o That no man is to be fined or imprisoned merely by the will of the state,
    but only by the judgement of his equals.

In 1956 Lord Devlin described the jury as the *"lamp that shows that freedom lives."*

Exam Questions on lay people

Magistrate :

1   Describe and explain the selection and appointment of law magistrates.
OCR AS Level Law, June 2003, Q1

2   Discuss the arguments for and against replacing lay magistrates with qualified lawyers.   *OCR AS Level Law, June 2004, Q7*

3   Describe the qualifications, selection and role of lay magistrates.
OCR AS Level Law, January 2006, Q3

Jury:

1   Describe the selection procedure of juries, including details of who cannot sit and who can be excused.   *OCR AS Level Law, June 2005, Q3*

2   Discuss the advantages and disadvantages of the system of jury selection.
OCR AS Level Law, January 2006, Q7

Lay people: both magistrates and juries:

1   (a)   Identify the courts, in which lay magistrates and juries sit and explain the roles of each in both criminal <u>and</u> civil cases.

     (b)   Discuss the advantages and disadvantages of using lay people as decision makers in courts.
OCR AS Level Law, June 2002, Q3

New specification specimen question: [see examples on pages 50, 63, 73, 78, 99]
The question, if on the paper, will be in the new format – example below:
(a)   **Describe** *(e.g. qualification, &/or selection, &/or role of magistrates &/or juries)*
     *… For **18 marks** … AO1*
(b)   **Discuss** *(comment upon detail given in answer to (a) above)*
     *….For **9 marks** …..AO2*   *[total 30 marks; AO3 worth 3]*

1   (a)   Describe the selection and training of lay magistrates.   [18]
     (b)   Discuss the advantages and disadvantages of using lay magistrates to make decisions in criminal matters.   [9] *[total 30 marks; AO3 worth 3]*
OCR AS Level Law,G141, June 2007, Q1

Ordinary men and women, with no legal qualifications, who play a crucial role in the decision making process in our courts – enabling public participation.
Justice is seen to be done: public confidence.

Ideally, suitable in character and integrity for the work they have to perform:
ability to assimilate factual information and make reasoned decision

o *You need to know:*
  o Where to receive advice and representation in civil and criminal cases
  o When one can receive government funding for legal fees for such advice
    & representation (means and merit tests – to qualify to receive funding).
  o Recent reform: Access to Justice Act 1999 [AJA 1999]
o *Need to be able to comment upon:*
  o Criteria for qualifying for government funding
  o Roles of LSC; CLS & CDS – and conditional fee agreements
  o Extent to which legal advice is available to everyone in civil & criminal cases
  o Whether, following the recent reforms, we now have access to justice for all.

* *

Difficulties in obtaining legal advice and representation:

o Lack of awareness of one's legal rights
o Feeling of intimidation of dealing with a lawyer
o Finding a lawyer close to home / work
o Cost of a lawyer: of obtaining advice and representation.

> **Limited access to free, independent legal advice**, for range of legal issues people encounter: e.g. divorce, debt and employment problems, personal injury and consumer issues and homelessness,

"The law courts of England are open to all men like the doors of the Ritz hotel"   **Mr Justice Darling**

It is the issue of :   **COST** and **AVAILABILITY** and **QUALITY** of **LEGAL ADVICE**,   (& REPRESENTATION in court) **that was the focus of the recent reform: AJA 1999.**

o Often referred to as the *"unmet legal need"* of society: lack of access to legal advice and representation, in order to solve problem.

o The government must balance:
  o **access to justice for all but at a cost**
  o **which government (taxpayer) can afford!**

If the law applies to everyone, then everyone should have Access to legal advice and assistance. – but cost to government rose by £529 million from 1992 – 1999! Also, it was not covering all deserving cases.

> ### AJA 1999:
>
> ❖ Replaced the old legal aid scheme with 2 new schemes:
> o **CLS** : Community Legal Service – for civil matters
> o **CDS** : Criminal Defence Service – for criminal matters
> ❖ *Both overseen by LSC* : **Legal Services Commission**.

LSC: Legal Services Commission:
- ❖ Since 1st April 2001 (AJA 1999) - replaced the Legal Aid Board
- ❖ **Aim: to improve quality and accessibility of legal services & tight control on budget.**
- ❖ Executive non-departmental public body
- ❖ Sponsored by the department of Constitutional Affairs
- ❖ Members of Commission are appointed by Lord Chancellor – *wide range of expertise and experience in legal services / advice sector / work of courts / consumer affairs.*

  - o Responsible for overseeing **funding** – in 2004, **budget** of £1.6 billion for year
  - o Decides Funding Code: criteria and procedure for civil and criminal case funding:
  - o i.e. <u>**sets criteria for CLS and CDS to follow in deciding if case can receive government funding for legal advise and representation**</u>.
  - o **Contracts** with solicitors/advice agencies – only those contracted with LSC can offer government funded advice / representation, & must meet quality mark to obtain contract. [to ensure quality of those who provide legally funded service.]
  - o Established **quality mark** – more informed choices for public
  - o Created **<u>website</u>** & <u>telephone helpline</u> - greater accessibility to information for public
  - o Create **network** of legal service providers – **partnerships** e.g. with Citizens Advice Bureaux; law centres.

Civil cases   - funding and advice

Government funding for legal fees has been available for civil matters since 1949.

Since AJA 1999:

- **FIXED BUDGET** each year for civil matters [Legal Service Fund – set by Lord Chancellor]
  - o *No longer demand-led*
    [i.e. a set limit after which is no money even if qualify for funding.]
  - o And, *more areas of civil law excluded from funding* :
    Personal Injury cases / business disputes.

- **Funding for civil matters is ADMINISTERED BY CLS: Community Legal Service**
  - o Applying funding code created by LSC.
  - o And "priority" of LSC: priority to cases of social welfare (housing, employment, benefit entitlements, debts); domestic violence; serious wrong-doing.
  - o **For ADVICE & REPRESENTATION BY SOLICITOR** (OR advice agencies) **WHO HAS CONTRACT WITH LSC.**
    ["franchised solicitors" – approx. 5,000 firms have contracts]
  - o **CLIENT** must **MEET CRITERIA** in funding code **IN ORDER TO QUALIFY** for legal funding.
    - o i.e. client must fulfil means / merit test, as required.

- **Legal help**
  - 2 hours initial advice and assistance with any legal problem
  - Means test

- **Legal Representation**
  - Full advice (preparation of case) & representation in court.
  - Means and Merit test.

Even if eligible for legal funding it is in form of a LOAN:
(statutory charge is applied to property recovered – repay funding to CLS.)

> For Family law disputes:
> Family Help and Family Mediation – funding for advice and representation at court (if needed)

> - *Help at court*
>   Advice and advocacy at court but without acting as legal representative in the proceedings. Means test.

Means Test -
Financial eligibility
Disposable income AND capital, of the client:

Disposable income: Income available after deductions
for housing costs, childcare
[min, of £279/month; max of £649/month]
(Gross income max. £2,350/month)

Disposable capital - Assets :
e.g. bank accounts, stocks & shares, jewellery and value of home (less amount of mortgage up to £100,000).
[min. of £3,000; max. of £8,000]

Lord Chancellor sets minimum and maximum limits each year for disposable income & capital.
Below the minimum
- client **qualifies for full legal funding**
Above the maximum
- client does **not qualify** for any legal funding
In between min. & max.
- client **qualifies for part-funding and** must pay **contribution** towards remainder of legal fees (contribution as % of amount above minimum figure set)

Merits Test
– likely success of the case
Plus: since AJA 1999 must also consider:
- Lord Chancellor's guidelines:

(wider test – harder to fulfil)

Lord Chancellor's guidelines:

- ❖ If damages will be more than costs
- ❖ Importance of matters for individual
- ❖ Availability of other services
- ❖ Conduct of the individual
- ❖ Public interest
- ❖ Amount of Community Legal Fund remaining

Conditional Fee Agreements – for civil cases

- **Agreement between client and solicitor**
- **Only pay solicitor's fee if win case**
- **However pay normal fee + "uplift fee"**
  - ○ "uplift fee" no more than 100% of normal fee and not more than 25% of damages won

- **If lose case not pay your solicitor's fees.**
- However, rule that losing party can be ordered to pay winner's costs remains.

- ❖ Take out insurance:
- If judge "awards costs" [order for the loser to pay the "winner's legal fees]
- insurance will cover these costs.
- AJA enables judge to include "uplift fee" and insurance premium paid, when "award costs"
    If win: pay your solicitor's fee + uplift fee
        [but may be paid by other party ("loser" or their insurance) if judge "award costs"]
    If lose: not pay your solicitor,
        [and your insurance pay other party's ("winner") legal fees if judge "awards costs"]

These "conditional fee agreements" have been available since CLSA 1990 for certain cases.
AJA 1999 extended availability to all civil cases (except family cases & medical negligence).
This enables individuals with case in area of civil law for which government funding is not available (e.g. personal injury), to be able still to have be able to have recourse to the courts without having to pay for a solicitor privately – without having to find the money upfront.

Disadvantages:

- ○ **Difficulty to find solicitor**: solicitors may only agree to conditional fee if they feel there is a good chance of winning – and only those cases where damages being sought are sufficient to cover their fee + uplift fee.
- ○ **The client still has to pay the insurance premium upfront**
- ○ **Criticism of allowing lawyers to have a financial interest** in the outcome of the case.
- ○ Criticism of **variation in "uplift fee" charged.**
- ○ **Insurance companies may exert pressure for individual to settle.**

Advantages:

- ○ **No cost for government**
- ○ **Increases availability of "access to justice"**: those ineligible for legal funding, or with case which is excluded from legal funding, can still bring or defend a civil court case, without expense of paying upfront - and only pay their solicitor if they win.
- ○ **Incentive for solicitor to win the case**

Evaluation of (AJA 1999) reform to civil funding/advice:

o **Greater control over quality**:
   o Contracts / quality mark

o **Greater accessibility**:
   o Website / partnerships with legal advice agencies [see below]
   o **But fewer solicitor firms made contract** (joined "franchise") (may have to travel to find one)
   o Increased availability of all solicitors to offer conditional fee agreement
      - **But many only offer if there is a good chance of success**
      - Is the only option for some cases: e.g. personal injury / inheritance
         disputes (not eligible for legal funding)
      - **Poorest clients not able to afford insurance premium**
      - Have been many challenges in enforceability of such agreements

> If legal funding is not obtainable; and no conditional fee agreement can be reached, then the only option is to pay privately for a solicitor or visit one of many legal advice centres. One can choose to represent oneself: "litigant in person".

o **BUT Further limited those who qualify for legal funding:**
o Select Committee on Constitutional Affairs reported in 2004 *"substantial risk that many people of modest means but who are home owners will fall out of the ambit of legal aid ... increasingly being restricted to those with no means at all"*

o Of those who do qualify for funding, many will pay **contribution** towards the funding;
o **A Statutory charge** may apply: repay funding to CLS out of damages/property if win.
o Even if qualify for legal funding – **can receive no funding if budget is used up!**
      [By civil cases or because funds transferred to fund criminal cases].

o Still general rule that legal funding is not available for Tribunals and forms of A.D.R [see p70 & 72]

Options:
[possible alternatives for problems of civil legal funding]

> **Create No-fault compensation** – for personal injury cases: then would be no need to go to court, not need to find solicitor willing to accept Conditional Fee agreement.

> **Create a National Legal Service** – a network of government employed lawyers to reduce costs of paying private contracted lawyers on case by case basis.

> **Enable "Class Actions"** – as seen in USA, where many individuals join in one case e.g. where many people have suffered same harm due to negligence of another person/company). This would reduce individual case costs.

Alternative for an individual: where to obtain free legal advice, other than from firm of solicitors.

CAB - Citizen's Advice Bureaux
– Began in 1938.

- Today approx. 1,000 throughout the country.
- Offer **free general advice and some legal advice.**
- Mainly cover **social and welfare problems; debts.**
- Reliant upon **volunteers** – but receive training – become expert in certain fields.
- Can **advise which local solicitors have contract** (with LSC) to offer government funded advice & representation; and those which offer reduced fixed-fee initial interview.
- **Often have a solicitor** on certain days.
- **Some have been awarded contracts by LSC** to provide government funded advice & some representation e.g. in small claims.
- **Funding is still difficult** to obtain – although improving with help from CLS (Community Legal Service)

LAW CENTRES.

- First opened in Kensington in 1970, to provide **free legal advice** in areas where there are few solicitors.
- Today ,the number of centres is growing following **funding by CLS** (Community Legal Service) & local authority
- Some centres have a duty solicitor scheme in the county court to deal with housing cases (e.g. issue of eviction).
- **Mainly cover housing, social and welfare,** employment, discrimination, and environmental problems.
- Open beyond office hours.
- Employ **lawyers and non-lawyers**
- Also run campaigns to raise public awareness of legal rights

Legal advice

TRADE UNIONS:
Offer legal advice for their members – e.g. employment problems.

CHARITIES:
Offer legal advice
e.g. the charity Shelter offers advice to anyone with a housing problem.

University: Some run "law Clinics" where students offer free advice, supervised by their tutors.

For Accidents:
1. **ALAS:** Law Society's Free Accident Legal Advice Service. Free initial interview by solicitors who are members of the scheme.
2. **AA and RAC :**   offer members help with traffic matters – car insurance companies

NOTE:
- *SOLICITORS:*
  - *Many offer **free or reduced-rate** fixed fee for **initial interview** (advertise &/or list with CAB).*
  - *Many offer Conditional-Fee agreements.*
- *BARRISTERS: (representation)*
  - *"pro-bono" work schemes have been running since 1992 – **free representation in court**. More than 2,000 cases a year are taken under this scheme.*

Options:
- ➤ Pay for solicitor, barrister
- ➤ Meet criteria for government funded solicitor, barrister; from those contracted with LSC.
- ➤ Find solicitor willing to make conditional fee agreement – (only for civil cases)
- ➤ Obtain advice from CAB or Law Centre … or free initial interview with solicitor; then represent yourself or find lawyer willing to undertake representation on "pro bono" basis.

Government funding for legal fees has been available for criminal matters since 1964.

Since AJA 1999:

Created **LSC** to oversee [see p83]; and
CDS: Criminal Defence Service - responsible for **funding** of criminal cases.

- **Still demand-led** : no set budget
- **Abolished means test for representation**– as only 1% were refused legal aid.
    - However, judge can order contribution be paid by defendant at end of trial.
- **Still duty solicitor schemes**
    - but now only firms with **contract** (franchise)
- **Introduced pilot scheme of salaried defenders**
- **Client must fulfil merits test, where required.**
- [Alternative is to hire / pay for solicitor oneself.]

Duty Solicitor Scheme

At police station & Magistrates' court.
Free Advice and Assistance.
No means or merit test.
No contribution – **free to all**
Duty Solicitor Rota Scheme – from those firms with **contract** with LSC.

> *but police discourage use of scheme, & quality varies - often advice from solicitor is by telephone; & cannot choose lawyer.*

Can cover <u>limited representation</u> in Magistrates' court:
- If is risk that defendant will be held in custody
- e.g. risk bail be denied / prison for non-payment of fine

(Initial) Advice and Assistance

one hour's work
Once charged, after leaving police station legal advice to help with negotiating with police, writing letters, how to prepare for case/trial.

Means test, [see p93] only those on low incomes will qualify however all can obtain free advice at police station / Magistrates' court under Duty Solicitor Scheme

---

Funded Advice and Representation
For trial / appeal. Apply to Magistrates' Clerk

MUST RECEIVE FUNDING FOR:
- Murder / prosecution appeal to HL / Bail issue whilst in custody

IN ALL OTHER CASES APPLY <u>MERITS TEST</u>:
Grant funding if "is in interests of justice" to do so
- Custodial sentence is likely
- Likely defendant will lose job *[note, is different merit test for criminal & civil]*
- Substantial questions of law to be argued
- Defendant is unable to follow proceedings
        (language barrier/mental ability)

However, judge can order contribution be paid by defendant at end of trial
Criminal Defence Bill will <u>reintroduce means test</u> and transfer application to LSC – currently apply to Magistrates' Clerk.
[due to ever increasing cost of criminal legal funding.]

Means test for legal representation in Mags' court re-introduced Oct 2006.
Funding now available only where D disposable income less than £20,000 & full funding if less than £12,000 – allowance for those on income support / under 18 in education …
Means Test likely be re-introduced Crown in 2007.

REPRESENTATION:

Under CDS, this is *provided from two areas*:

> Criticism that public defender may lack impartiality – as is government employed.

1. <u>**Lawyers in private practice**</u> who have a contract with the LSC

2. Government employed lawyers: <u>**PDS: Public Defender Service**</u>

The PDS was set up (under AJA 1999) as a pilot scheme with 4 offices (now there are 8), to provide independent, high quality & value for money criminal defence services to the public. The idea is to ensure availability of representation; but with the aim of reducing the ever-increasing costs of government funding of criminal cases by **using employed lawyers as benchmark to check that fees charged by private practice lawyers are reasonable**. Individual can choose between private lawyer (pay or government funded) or PDS lawyer.

❖ However, the PDS has proved expensive: running costs were over £10 million in 2003/4.
❖ **criticism is that individuals will be both prosecuted and defended by a government agency**

Summary of AJA 1999 reforms:
to government legal funding (for advice & representation)

1. BUDGET
- **Capped (limit) for civil cases** (this limits the number of cases which can receive funding)
- No change to criminal budget – still fund all cases which qualify

2. FRANCHISE
- **Takes idea of franchise further**:
  Today, only those solicitors / barristers who have contract with LSC can offer government funded work.
- **Introduction of government public defenders** for criminal cases [PDS]

3. ELIGIBILITY
- **New merits test for civil cases** – wider, harder to fulfil
- **Fewer areas of civil law where government funding is available**: exclusion of personal injury and business disputes results in loss of availability of legal advice & representation in these areas unless can afford to pay lawyer or find one who will accept Conditional Fee agreement.
- **Abolished means test for representation in criminal cases**.
  Alongside increased use of lay advisers for civil matters (advice agencies) – yet no quality control.

Exam Questions on legal funding and advice

CIVIL :

1. Describe the different ways of obtaining representation in civil cases, including conditional fee agreements.
    OCR AS Level Law, January 2005, Q3

2. Abim wants to bring a claim in the civil courts.
    Discuss the advantages and disadvantages of the different ways in which he may obtain representation.
    OCR AS Level Law, January 2006, Q6

3. Discuss the extent to which legal advice is available to everyone who has a legal problem in a civil matter.
    OCR AS Level Law, June 2003, Q6

CRIMINAL:

1. Describe the different types of legal help and representation available from the Criminal Defence Service.
    OCR AS Level Law, June 2003, Q4

Both: civil and criminal

1. Explain the different ways of obtaining legal advice on **both** civil **and** criminal matters. (Do not include representation)
    OCR AS Level Law, January 2006, Q2

New specification specimen question: [see examples on pages 50, 63, 73, 78,]

The question, if on the paper, will be in the new format – example below:

(a) **Describe**

(e.g. availability of funding and advice &/or representation, for civil &/or criminal cases)
*… For **18 marks** … AO1*

(b) **Discuss**

(comment upon detail given in answer to (a) above
*e.g. the advantages & disadvantages of the AJA 1999 reforms with regards to civil &/or criminal matters … status of access to justice today) …. For **9 marks** ….. AO2*

[total 30 marks; AO3 worth 3]

1. (a) Describe conditional fee arrangements and publicly funded legal representation in civil cases. [18]

    (b) Discuss the problems of conditional fee agreements. [9]

    QWC [3]; Total marks [30]
    OCR AS Level Law, G141, January 2007, Q4

Printed in the United Kingdom by
Lightning Source UK Ltd., Milton Keynes
136807UK00001B/133-146/P